THE GOSPEL OF LIFE

[*EVANGELIUM VITAE*]

POPE JOHN PAUL II

Published by Random House Large Print
in association with Times Books,
a division of Random House, Inc.
New York 1995

PUBLISHER'S NOTE:
This edition of *The Gospel of Life*
[*Evangelium Vitae*], in the
official English translation provided by
the Vatican, contains
the integral and correct text of
the Encyclical Letter given
in Rome, at Saint Peter's, on March 25, 1995, the
seventeenth year of the Pontificate of John Paul II.
Not one word has been omitted.

Published in the United States of America by
Random House Large Print
in association with Times Books,
a division of Random House, Inc., New York,
and simultaneously in Canada by
Random House of Canada Limited,
Toronto.
Distributed by Random House, Inc., New York.

Manufactured in the United States of America
FIRST LARGE PRINT EDITION

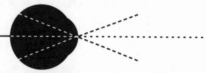

This Large Print Book carries the
Seal of Approval of N.A.V.H.

THE GOSPEL OF LIFE

CONTENTS

INTRODUCTION 3

The incomparable worth of the human person [2]   4

New threats to human life [3–4] 6

In communion with all the Bishops of the world
[5–6] 10

CHAPTER I

THE VOICE OF YOUR BROTHER'S BLOOD
CRIES TO ME FROM THE GROUND
Present-Day Threats to Human Life

"Cain rose up against his brother Abel, and
killed him" (*Gen* 4:8): the roots of violence
against life [7–9] 15

"What have you done?" (*Gen* 4:10): the eclipse
of the value of life [10–17] 22

"Am I my brother's keeper?" (*Gen* 4:9): a perverse idea of freedom [18–20] 35

"And from your face I shall be hidden" (*Gen*
4:14): the eclipse of the sense of God and of
man [21–24] 44

"You have come to the sprinkled blood" (cf.
Heb 12:22, 24): signs of hope and invitation
to commitment [25–28] 51

CHAPTER II
I CAME THAT THEY MAY HAVE LIFE
The Christian Message Concerning Life

"The life was made manifest, and we saw it" (*1 Jn* 1:2): with our gaze fixed on Christ, "the Word of life" [29–30]. 61

"The Lord is my strength and my song, and he has become my salvation" (*Ex* 15:2): life is always a good [31] 64

"The name of Jesus . . . has made this man strong" (*Acts* 3:16): in the uncertainties of human life, Jesus brings life's meaning to fulfilment [32–33] 66

"Called . . . to be conformed to the image of his Son" (*Rom* 8:28–29): God's glory shines on the face of man [34–36] 71

"Whoever lives and believes in me shall never die" (*Jn* 11:26): the gift of eternal life [37–38] 77

"From man in regard to his fellow man I will demand an accounting" (*Gen* 9:5): reverence and love for every human life [39–41] 80

"Be fruitful and multiply, and fill the earth and subdue it" (*Gen* 1:28): man's responsibility for life [42–43] 85

"For you formed my inmost being" (*Ps* 139:13): the dignity of the unborn child [44–45] . . 90

"I kept my faith even when I said, 'I am greatly afflicted' " (*Ps* 116:10): life in old age and at times of suffering [46–47] 94

"All who hold her fast will live" (*Bar* 4:1): from
the law of Sinai to the gift of the Spirit
[48–49]   97
"They shall look on him whom they have
pierced" (*Jn* 19:37): the Gospel of life is
brought to fulfilment on the tree of the Cross
[50–51]   102

CHAPTER III
YOU SHALL NOT KILL
God's Holy Law

"If you would enter life, keep the commandments" (*Mt* 19:17): Gospel and commandment [52]   107
"From man in regard to his fellow man I will
demand an accounting for human life" (*Gen*
9:5): human life is sacred and inviolable [53–
57]   110
"Your eyes beheld my unformed substance" (*Ps*
139:16): the unspeakable crime of abortion
[58–63]   119
"It is I who bring both death and life" (*Dt*
32:39): the tragedy of euthanasia [64–67] .   132
"We must obey God rather than men" (*Acts*
5:29): civil law and the moral law [68–74]   141
"You shall love your neighbour as yourself" (*Lk*
10:27): "promote" life [75–77]   156

CHAPTER IV
YOU DID IT TO ME
For a New Culture of Human Life

"You are God's own people, that you may declare the wonderful deeds of him who called
you out of darkness into his marvellous
light" (*1 Pet* 2:9): a people of life and for life
[78–79]   161
"That which we have seen and heard we proclaim also to you" (*1 Jn* 1:3): proclaiming
the Gospel of life [80–82]   164
"I give you thanks that I am fearfully, wonder-
fully made" (*Ps* 139:14): celebrating the
Gospel of life [83–86].   169
"What does it profit, my brethren, if a man says
he has faith but has not works?" (*Jas* 2:14):
serving the Gospel of life [87–91]   176
"Your children will be like olive shoots around
your table" (*Ps* 128:3): the family as the
"sanctuary of life" [92–94]   187
"Walk as children of light" (*Eph* 5:8): bringing
about a transformation of culture [95–100]   192
"We are writing this that our joy may be complete" (*1 Jn* 1:4): the Gospel of life is for the
whole of human society [101–102]   204

CONCLUSION   207
"A great portent appeared in heaven, a woman
clothed with the sun" (*Rev* 12:1): the motherhood of Mary and of the Church [103] . .   208

"And the dragon stood before the woman . . .
that he might devour her child when she
brought it forth" (*Rev* 12:4): life menaced
by the forces of evil [104] 211
"Death shall be no more" (*Rev* 21:4): the splendour of the Resurrection [105] 212

NOTES 217

ENCYCLICAL LETTER
EVANGELIUM VITAE
ADDRESSED BY THE SUPREME PONTIFF
JOHN PAUL II
TO THE BISHOPS
PRIESTS AND DEACONS
MEN AND WOMEN RELIGIOUS
LAY FAITHFUL
AND ALL PEOPLE OF GOOD WILL
ON THE VALUE AND INVIOLABILITY
OF HUMAN LIFE

INTRODUCTION

1.   THE GOSPEL OF LIFE is at the heart of Jesus' message. Lovingly received day after day by the Church, it is to be preached with dauntless fidelity as "good news" to the people of every age and culture.

At the dawn of salvation, it is the Birth of a Child which is proclaimed as joyful news: "I bring you good news of a great joy which will come to all the people; for to you is born this day in the city of David a Saviour, who is Christ the Lord" (*Lk* 2:10-11). The source of this "great joy" is the Birth of the Saviour; but Christmas also reveals the full meaning of every human birth, and the joy which accompanies the Birth of the Messiah is thus seen to be the foundation and fulfilment of joy at every child born into the world (cf. *Jn* 16:21).

When he presents the heart of his redemptive mission, Jesus says: "I came that they may have life, and have it abundantly" (*Jn* 10:10). In truth, he is referring to that "new" and "eternal" life which consists in communion with the Father, to which every person is freely called in the Son by the power of the Sanctifying Spirit. It is precisely in this "life" that all the aspects and stages of human life achieve their full significance.

The incomparable worth of the human person

2.   Man is called to a fullness of life which far exceeds the dimensions of his earthly existence, because it consists in sharing the very life of God. The loftiness of this supernatural vocation reveals the *greatness* and the *inestimable value* of human life even in its temporal phase. Life in time, in fact; is the fundamental condition, the initial stage and an integral part of the entire unified process of human existence. It is a process which, unexpectedly and undeservedly, is enlightened by the promise and renewed by the gift of divine life, which will reach its full realization in eternity (cf. *1 Jn* 3:1-2). At the same time, it is precisely this supernatural calling which highlights the *relative character* of each individual's earthly life. After all, life on earth is not an "ultimate" but a "penultimate" reality; even so, it remains a *sacred reality* entrusted to us, to be preserved with a sense of responsibility and brought to perfection in love

and in the gift of ourselves to God and to our brothers and sisters.

The Church knows that this *Gospel of life,* which she has received from her Lord,[1] has a profound and persuasive echo in the heart of every person—believer and non-believer alike—because it marvellously fulfils all the heart's expectations while infinitely surpassing them. Even in the midst of difficulties and uncertainties, every person sincerely open to truth and goodness can, by the light of reason and the hidden action of grace, come to recognize in the natural law written in the heart (cf. *Rom* 2:14-15) the sacred value of human life from its very beginning until its end, and can affirm the right of every human being to have this primary good respected to the highest degree. Upon the recognition of this right, every human community and the political community itself are founded.

In a special way, believers in Christ must defend and promote this right, aware as they are of the wonderful truth recalled by the Second Vatican Council: "By his incarnation the Son of God has united himself in some fashion with every human being".[2] This saving event reveals to humanity not only the boundless love of God who "so loved the world that he gave his only

Son'' (*Jn* 3:16), but also the *incomparable value of every human person.*

The Church, faithfully contemplating the mystery of the Redemption, acknowledges this value with ever new wonder.3 She feels called to proclaim to the people of all times this "Gospel", the source of invincible hope and true joy for every period of history. *The Gospel of God's love for man, the Gospel of the dignity of the person and the Gospel of life are a single and indivisible Gospel.*

For this reason, man—living man—represents the primary and fundamental way for the Church.4

New threats to human life

3.   Every individual, precisely by reason of the mystery of the Word of God who was made flesh (cf. *Jn* 1:14), is entrusted to the maternal care of the Church. Therefore every threat to human dignity and life must necessarily be felt in the Church's very heart; it cannot but affect her at the core of her faith in the Redemptive Incarnation of the Son of God, and engage her in her mission of proclaiming the *Gospel of life* in all the world and to every creature (cf. *Mk* 16:15).

Today this proclamation is especially pressing because of the extraordinary increase and gravity of threats to the life of individuals and peoples, especially where life is weak and defenceless. In addition to the ancient scourges of poverty, hunger, endemic diseases, violence and war, new threats are emerging on an alarmingly vast scale.

The Second Vatican Council, in a passage which retains all its relevance today, forcefully condemned a number of crimes and attacks against human life. Thirty years later, taking up the words of the Council and with the same forcefulness I repeat that condemnation in the name of the whole Church, certain that I am interpreting the genuine sentiment of every upright conscience: "Whatever is opposed to life itself, such as any type of murder, genocide, abortion, euthanasia, or wilful self-destruction, whatever violates the integrity of the human person, such as mutilation, torments inflicted on body or mind, attempts to coerce the will itself; whatever insults human dignity, such as subhuman living conditions, arbitrary imprisonment, deportation, slavery, prostitution, the selling of women and children; as well as disgraceful working conditions, where people are treated as mere instruments of gain rather than as free and responsible persons; all these things and others like them are infamies indeed. They poison human society, and they do more harm to those who practise them than to those who suffer from the injury. Moreover, they are a supreme dishonour to the Creator''.5

4.   Unfortunately, this disturbing state of affairs, far from decreasing, is expanding: with the new prospects opened up by scientific and technological progress there arise new forms of attacks on the dignity of the human being. At the same time a new cultural climate is developing and taking hold, which gives crimes against life a *new and—if possible—even more sinister character,* giving rise to further grave concern: broad sectors of public opinion justify certain crimes against life in the name of the rights of individual freedom, and on this basis they claim not only exemption from punishment but even authorization by the State, so that these things can be done with total freedom and indeed with the free assistance of health-care systems.

All this is causing a profound change in the way in which life and relationships between people are considered. The fact that legislation in many countries, perhaps even departing from basic principles of their Constitutions, has determined not to punish these practices against life, and even to make them altogether legal, is both a disturbing symptom and a significant cause of grave moral decline. Choices once unanimously considered criminal and rejected by the common moral sense are gradually becoming socially acceptable. Even certain sectors of the medical profession, which by its calling is directed to the defence and care of human life, are increasingly willing to carry out these acts against the person. In this way the very nature of the medical profession is distorted and contradicted, and the dignity of those who practise it is degraded. In such a cultural and legislative situation, the serious demographic, social and family problems which weigh upon many of the world's peoples and which require responsible and effective attention from national and international bodies, are left open to false and deceptive solutions, opposed to the truth and the good of persons and nations.

The end result of this is tragic: not only is the fact of the destruction of so many human lives still to be born or in their final stage extremely grave and disturbing, but no less grave and disturbing is the fact that conscience itself, darkened as it were by such widespread conditioning, is finding it increasingly difficult to distinguish between good and evil in what concerns the basic value of human life.

In communion with all the Bishops of the world

5.   The *Extraordinary Consistory* of Cardinals held in Rome on 4-7 April 1991 was devoted to the problem of the threats to human life in our day. After a thorough and detailed discussion of the problem and of the challenges it poses to the entire human family and in particular to the Christian community, the Cardinals unanimously asked me to reaffirm with the authority of the Successor of Peter the value of human life and its inviolability, in the light of present circumstances and attacks threatening it today.

In response to this request, at Pentecost in 1991 I wrote a *personal letter* to each of my Brother Bishops asking them, in the spirit of episcopal collegiality, to offer me their cooperation in drawing up a specific document.[6] I am deeply grateful to all the Bishops who replied and provided me with valuable facts, suggestions and proposals. In so doing they bore witness to their unanimous desire to share in the doctrinal and pastoral mission of the Church with regard to the *Gospel of life*.

In that same letter, written shortly after the celebration of the centenary of the Encyclical *Rerum Novarum*, I drew everyone's attention to this striking analogy: "Just as a century ago it was the working classes which were oppressed in their fundamental rights, and the Church very courageously came to their defence by proclaiming the sacrosanct rights of the worker as a person, so now, when another category of persons is being oppressed in the fundamental right to life, the Church feels in duty bound to speak out with the same courage on behalf of those who have no voice. Hers is always the evangelical cry in defence of the world's poor, those who are threatened and despised and whose human rights are violated".[7]

Today there exists a great multitude of weak and defenceless human beings, unborn children in particular, whose fundamental right to life is being trampled upon. If, at the end of the last century, the Church could not be silent about the injustices of those times, still less can she be silent today, when the social injustices of the past, unfortunately not yet overcome, are being compounded in many regions of the world by still more grievous forms of injustice and oppression, even if these are being presented as elements of progress in view of a new world order.

The present Encyclical, the fruit of the cooperation of the Episcopate of every country of the world, is therefore meant to be a *precise and vigorous reaffirmation of the value of human life and its inviolability,* and at the same time a pressing appeal addressed to each and every person, in the name of God: *respect, protect, love and serve life, every human life!* Only in this direction will you find justice, development, true freedom, peace and happiness!

May these words reach all the sons and daughters of the Church! May they reach all people of good will who are concerned for the good of every man and woman and for the destiny of the whole of society!

6.   In profound communion with all my brothers and sisters in the faith, and inspired by genuine friendship towards all, I wish to *meditate upon once more and proclaim the Gospel of life,* the splendour of truth which enlightens consciences, the clear light which corrects the darkened gaze, and the unfailing source of faithfulness and steadfastness in facing the ever new challenges which we meet along our path.

As I recall the powerful experience of the Year of the Family, as if to complete the *Letter* which I wrote "to every particular family in every part of the world",[8] I look with renewed confidence to every household and I pray that at every level a general commitment to support the family will reappear and be strengthened, so that today too—even amid so many difficulties and serious threats—the family will always remain, in accordance with God's plan, the "sanctuary of life".9

To all the members of the Church, *the people of life and for life,* I make this most urgent appeal, that together we may offer this world of ours new signs of hope, and work to ensure that justice and solidarity will increase and that a new culture of human life will be affirmed, for the building of an authentic civilization of truth and love.

CHAPTER I

THE VOICE
OF YOUR BROTHER'S BLOOD
CRIES TO ME FROM THE GROUND

PRESENT-DAY THREATS TO HUMAN LIFE

"Cain rose up against his brother Abel, and killed him" (Gen 4:8): the roots of violence against life

7.   "God did not make death, and he does not delight in the death of the living. For he has created all things that they might exist . . . *God created man for incorruption,* and made him in the image of his own eternity, but through the devil's envy *death entered the world,* and those who belong to his party experience it" (*Wis* 1:13-14; 2:23-24).

The Gospel of life, proclaimed in the beginning when man was created in the image of God for a destiny of full and perfect life (cf. *Gen* 2:7; *Wis* 9:2-3), is contradicted by the painful experience of *death which enters the world* and casts its shadow of meaninglessness over man's entire existence. Death came into the world as a result

15

of the devil's envy (cf. *Gen* 3:1,4-5) and the sin of our first parents (cf. *Gen* 2:17, 3:17-19). And death entered it in a violent way, *through the killing of Abel by his brother Cain:* "And when they were in the field, Cain rose up against his brother Abel, and killed him" (*Gen* 4:8).

This first murder is presented with singular eloquence in a page of the Book of Genesis which has universal significance: it is a page rewritten daily, with inexorable and degrading frequency, in the book of human history.

Let us re-read together this biblical account which, despite its archaic structure and its extreme simplicity, has much to teach us.

"Now Abel was a keeper of sheep, and Cain a tiller of the ground. In the course of time Cain brought to the Lord an offering of the fruit of the ground, and Abel brought of the firstlings of his flock and of their fat portions. And the Lord had regard for Abel and his offering, but for Cain and his offering he had not regard. So Cain was very angry, and his countenance fell. The Lord said to Cain, 'Why are you angry and why has your countenance fallen? If you do well, will you not be accepted? And if you do not do well, sin is crouching at the door; its desire is for you, but you must master it'.

"Cain said to Abel his brother, 'Let us go

out to the field'. And when they were in the field, Cain rose up against his brother Abel, and killed him. Then the Lord said to Cain, 'Where is Abel your brother?' He said, 'I do not know; am I my brother's keeper?' And the Lord said, 'What have you done? The voice of your brother's blood is crying to me from the ground. And now you are cursed from the ground, which has opened its mouth to receive your brother's blood from your hand. When you till the ground, it shall no longer yield to you its strength; you shall be a fugitive and a wanderer on the earth'. Cain said to the Lord, 'My punishment is greater than I can bear. Behold, you have driven me this day away from the ground; and from your face I shall be hidden; and I shall be a fugitive and a wanderer on the earth, and whoever finds me will slay me'. Then the Lord said to him, 'Not so! If any one slays Cain, vengeance shall be taken on him sevenfold'. And the Lord put a mark on Cain, lest any who came upon him should kill him. Then Cain went away from the presence of the Lord, and dwelt in the land of Nod, east of Eden" (Gen 4:2-16).

8.   Cain was "very angry" and his countenance "fell" because "the Lord had regard for Abel and his offering" (*Gen* 4:4-5). The biblical

text does not reveal the reason why God prefers Abel's sacrifice to Cain's. It clearly shows however that God, although preferring Abel's gift, *does not interrupt his dialogue with Cain.* He admonishes him, *reminding him of his freedom in the face of evil:* man is in no way predestined to evil. Certainly, like Adam, he is tempted by the malevolent force of sin which, like a wild beast, lies in wait at the door of his heart, ready to leap on its prey. But Cain remains free in the face of sin. He can and must overcome it: "Its desire is for you, but you must master it" (*Gen* 4:7).

Envy and anger have the upper hand over the Lord's warning, and so Cain attacks his own brother and kills him. As we read in the *Catechism of the Catholic Church:* "In the account of Abel's murder by his brother Cain, Scripture reveals the presence of anger and envy in man, consequences of original sin, from the beginning of human history. Man has become the enemy of his fellow man".[10]

Brother kills brother. Like the first fratricide, every murder is a violation of the *"spiritual" kinship* uniting mankind in one great family,[11] in which all share the same fundamental good: equal personal dignity. Not infrequently the *kinship "of flesh and blood"* is also violated; for example when threats to life arise within the relationship between parents and children, such as happens in abortion or when, in the wider context of family or kinship, euthanasia is encouraged or practised.

At the root of every act of violence against one's neighbour there is *a concession to the "thinking" of the evil one,* the one who "was a murderer from the beginning" (*Jn* 8:44). As the Apostle John reminds us: "For this is the message which you have heard from the beginning, that we should love one another, and not be like Cain who was of the evil one and murdered his brother" (*1 Jn* 3:11-12). Cain's killing of his brother at the very dawn of history is thus a sad witness of how evil spreads with amazing speed: man's revolt against God in the earthly paradise is followed by the deadly combat of man against man.

After the crime, *God intervenes to avenge the one killed.* Before God, who asks him about the fate of Abel, Cain, instead of showing remorse and apologizing, arrogantly eludes the question: "I do not know; am I my brother's keeper?" (*Gen* 4:9). *"I do not know":* Cain tries to cover up his crime with a lie. This was and still is the case, when all kinds of ideologies try to justify and disguise the most atrocious crimes against human beings. *"Am I my brother's keeper?":* Cain does not wish to think about his brother and refuses to accept the responsibility which every person has towards others. We cannot but think of today's tendency for people to refuse to accept responsibility for their brothers and sisters Symptoms of this trend include the lack of solidarity towards society's weakest members—such as the elderly, the infirm, immigrants, children—and the indifference frequently found in relations between the world's peoples even when basic values such as survival, freedom and peace are involved.

9.   But *God cannot leave the crime unpunished:* from the ground on which it has been spilt, the blood of the one murdered demands that God should render justice (cf. *Gen* 37:26; *Is* 26:21; *Ez* 24:7-8). From this text the Church has taken the name of the "sins which cry to God for justice", and, first among them, she has included wilful murder.[12] For the Jewish people, as for many peoples of antiquity, blood is the source of life. Indeed "the blood is the life" (*Dt* 12:23), and life, especially human life, belongs only to God: for this reason *whoever attacks human life, in some way attacks God himself.*

Cain is cursed by God and also by the earth, which will deny him its fruit (cf. *Gen* 4:12). *He is punished:* he will live in the wilderness and the desert. Murderous violence profoundly changes man's environment. From being the "garden of Eden" (*Gen* 2:15), a place of plenty, of harmonious interpersonal relationships and of friendship with God, the earth becomes "the land of Nod" (*Gen* 4:16), a place of scarcity, loneliness and separation from God. Cain will be "a fugitive and a wanderer on the earth" (*Gen* 4:14): uncertainty and restlessness will follow him forever.

And yet God, who is always merciful even when he punishes, *"put a mark on Cain,* lest any who came upon him should kill him" (*Gen* 4:15). He thus gave him a distinctive sign, not to condemn him to the hatred of others, but to protect and defend him from those wishing to kill him, even out of a desire to avenge Abel's death. *Not even a murderer loses his personal dignity,* and God himself pledges to guarantee this. And it is precisely here that the *paradoxical mystery of the merciful justice of God* is shown forth. As Saint Ambrose writes: "Once the crime is admitted at the very inception of this sinful act of parricide, then the divine law of God's mercy should be immediately extended. If punishment is forthwith inflicted on the accused, then men in the exercise of justice would in no way observe patience and moderation, but would straightaway condemn the defendant to punishment. . . . God drove Cain out of his presence and sent him into exile far away from his native land, so that he passed from a life of human kindness to one which was more akin to the rude existence of a wild beast. God, who preferred the correction rather than the death of a sinner, did not desire that a homicide be punished by the exaction of another act of homicide''.[13]

"What have you done?" (Gen 4:10): the eclipse of the value of life

10.   The Lord said to Cain: "What have you done? The voice of your brother's blood is crying to me from the ground" (*Gen* 4:10). *The voice of the blood shed by men continues to cry out,* from generation to generation, in ever new and different ways.

The Lord's question: "What have you done?", which Cain cannot escape, is addressed also to the people of today, to make them realize the extent and gravity of the attacks against life which continue to mark human history; to make them discover what causes these attacks and feeds them; and to make them ponder seriously the consequences which derive from these attacks for the existence of individuals and peoples.

Some threats come from nature itself, but

they are made worse by the culpable indifference and negligence of those who could in some cases remedy them. Others are the result of situations of violence, hatred and conflicting interests, which lead people to attack others through murder, war, slaughter and genocide.

And how can we fail to consider the violence against life done to millions of human beings, especially children, who are forced into poverty, malnutrition and hunger because of an unjust distribution of resources between peoples and between social classes? And what of the violence inherent not only in wars as such but in the scandalous arms trade, which spawns the many armed conflicts which stain our world with blood? What of the spreading of death caused by reckless tampering with the world's ecological balance, by the criminal spread of drugs, or by the promotion of certain kinds of sexual activity which, besides being morally unacceptable, also involve grave risks to life? It is impossible to catalogue completely the vast array of threats to human life, so many are the forms, whether explicit or hidden, in which they appear today!

11.   Here though we shall concentrate particular attention on *another category of attacks,* affecting life in its earliest and in its final stages,

attacks which present *new characteristics with respect to the past and which raise questions of extraordinary seriousness*. It is not only that in generalized opinion these attacks tend no longer to be considered as "crimes"; paradoxically they assume the nature of "rights", to the point that the State is called upon to give them *legal recognition and to make them available through the free services of health-care personnel*. Such attacks strike human life at the time of its greatest frailty, when it lacks any means of self-defence. Even more serious is the fact that, most often, those attacks are carried out in the very heart of and with the complicity of the family—the family which by its nature is called to be the "sanctuary of life".

How did such a situation come about? Many different factors have to be taken into account. In the background there is the profound crisis of culture, which generates scepticism in relation to the very foundations of knowledge and ethics, and which makes it increasingly difficult to grasp clearly the meaning of what man is, the meaning of his rights and his duties. Then there are all kinds of existential and interpersonal difficulties, made worse by the complexity of a society in which individuals, couples and families are often left alone with their problems. There are situations of acute poverty, anxiety or frustration in which the struggle to make ends meet, the presence of unbearable pain, or instances of violence, especially against women, make the choice to defend and promote life so demanding as sometimes to reach the point of heroism.

All this explains, at least in part, how the value of life can today undergo a kind of "eclipse", even though conscience does not cease to point to it as a sacred and inviolable value, as is evident in the tendency to disguise certain crimes against life in its early or final stages by using innocuous medical terms which distract attention from the fact that what is involved is the right to life of an actual human person.

12.   In fact, while the climate of widespread moral uncertainty can in some way be explained by the multiplicity and gravity of today's social problems, and these can sometimes mitigate the subjective responsibility of individuals, it is no less true that we are confronted by an even larger reality, which can be described as a veritable *structure of sin*. This reality is characterized by the emergence of a culture which denies solidarity and in many cases takes the form of a veritable "culture of death". This culture is actively fos-

tered by powerful cultural, economic and political currents which encourage an idea of society excessively concerned with efficiency. Looking at the situation from this point of view, it is possible to speak in a certain sense of a *war of the powerful against the weak:* a life which would require greater acceptance, love and care is considered useless, or held to be an intolerable burden, and is therefore rejected in one way or another. A person who, because of illness, handicap or, more simply, just by existing, compromises the well-being or life-style of those who are more favoured tends to be looked upon as an enemy to be resisted or eliminated. In this way a kind of *"conspiracy against life"* is unleashed. This conspiracy involves not only individuals in their personal, family or group relationships, but goes far beyond, to the point of damaging and distorting, at the international level, relations between peoples and States.

13.   In order to facilitate the spread of *abortion,* enormous sums of money have been invested and continue to be invested in the production of pharmaceutical products which make it possible to kill the fetus in the mother's womb without recourse to medical assistance. On this point, scientific research itself seems to be

almost exclusively preoccupied with developing products which are ever more simple and effective in suppressing life and which at the same time are capable of removing abortion from any kind of control or social responsibility.

It is frequently asserted that *contraception,* if made safe and available to all, is the most effective remedy against abortion. The Catholic Church is then accused of actually promoting abortion, because she obstinately continues to teach the moral unlawfulness of contraception. When looked at carefully, this objection is clearly unfounded. It may be that many people use contraception with a view to excluding the subsequent temptation of abortion. But the negative values inherent in the "contraceptive mentality" —which is very different from responsible parenthood, lived in respect for the full truth of the conjugal act—are such that they in fact strengthen this temptation when an unwanted life is conceived. Indeed, the pro-abortion culture is especially strong precisely where the Church's teaching on contraception is rejected. Certainly, from the moral point of view contraception and abortion are *specifically different* evils: the former contradicts the full truth of the sexual act as the proper expression of conjugal love, while the latter destroys the life of a human being; the former is opposed to the virtue of chastity in marriage, the latter is opposed to the virtue of justice and directly violates the divine commandment "You shall not kill".

But despite their differences of nature and moral gravity, contraception and abortion are often closely connected, as fruits of the same tree. It is true that in many cases contraception and even abortion are practised under the pressure of real-life difficulties, which nonetheless can never exonerate from striving to observe God's law fully. Still, in very many other instances such practices are rooted in a hedonistic mentality unwilling to accept responsibility in matters of sexuality, and they imply a self-centered concept of freedom, which regards procreation as an obstacle to personal fulfilment. The life which could result from a sexual encounter thus becomes an enemy to be avoided at all costs, and abortion becomes the only possible decisive response to failed contraception.

The close connection which exists, in mentality, between the practice of contraception and that of abortion is becoming increasingly obvious. It is being demonstrated in an alarming way by the development of chemical products, intra-uterine devices and vaccines which, distributed with the same ease as contraceptives, really act as abortifacients in the very early stages of the development of the life of the new human being.

14.   The various *techniques of artificial reproduction,* which would seem to be at the service of life and which are frequently used with this intention, actually open the door to new threats against life. Apart from the fact that they are morally unacceptable, since they separate procreation from the fully human context of the conjugal act,[14] these techniques have a high rate of failure: not just failure in relation to fertilization but with regard to the subsequent development of the embryo, which is exposed to the risk of death, generally within a very short space of time. Furthermore, the number of embryos produced is often greater than that needed for implantation in the woman's womb, and these so-called "spare embryos" are then destroyed or used for research which, under the pretext of scientific or medical progress, in fact reduces human life to the level of simple "biological material" to be freely disposed of.

Prenatal diagnosis, which presents no moral objections if carried out in order to identify the medical treatment which may be needed by the child in the womb, all too often becomes an opportunity for proposing and procuring an abortion. This is eugenic abortion, justified in public opinion on the basis of a mentality—mistakenly held to be consistent with the demands of "therapeutic interventions"—which accepts life only under certain conditions and rejects it when it is affected by any limitation, handicap or illness.

Following this same logic, the point has been reached where the most basic care, even nourishment, is denied to babies born with serious handicaps or illnesses. The contemporary scene, moreover, is becoming even more alarming by reason of the proposals, advanced here and there, to justify even *infanticide,* following the same arguments used to justify the right to abortion. In this way, we revert to a state of barbarism which one hoped had been left behind forever.

15.   Threats which are no less serious hang over the *incurably ill* and the *dying.* In a social and cultural context which makes it more difficult to face and accept suffering, the *temptation* becomes all the greater *to resolve the problem of suffering by eliminating it at the root,* by hastening death so that it occurs at the moment considered most suitable.

Various considerations usually contribute to such a decision, all of which converge in the same terrible outcome. In the sick person the sense of anguish, of severe discomfort, and even of desperation brought on by intense and prolonged suffering can be a decisive factor. Such a situation can threaten the already fragile equilibrium of an individual's personal and family life, with the result that, on the one hand, the sick person, despite the help of increasingly effective medical and social assistance, risks feeling overwhelmed by his or her own frailty; and on the other hand, those close to the sick person can be moved by an understandable even if misplaced compassion. All this is aggravated by a cultural climate which fails to perceive any meaning or value in suffering, but rather considers suffering the epitome of evil, to be eliminated at all costs. This is especially the case in the absence of a religious outlook which could help to provide a positive understanding of the mystery of suffering.

On a more general level, there exists in contemporary culture a certain Promethean attitude which leads people to think that they can control life and death by taking the decisions about them into their own hands. What really happens in this case is that the individual is overcome and crushed by a death deprived of any prospect of meaning or hope. We see a tragic expression of all this in the spread of *euthanasia*—disguised and surreptitious, or practised openly and even legally. As well as for reasons of a misguided pity at the sight of the patient's suffering, euthanasia is sometimes justified by the utilitarian motive of avoiding costs which bring no return and which weigh heavily on society. Thus it is proposed to eliminate malformed babies, the severely handicapped, the disabled, the elderly, especially when they are not self-sufficient, and the terminally ill. Nor can we remain silent in the face of other more furtive, but no less serious and real, forms of euthanasia. These could occur for example when, in order to increase the availability of organs for transplants, organs are removed without respecting objective and adequate criteria which verify the death of the donor.

16.   Another present-day *phenomenon,* frequently used to justify threats and attacks against life, is the *demographic* question. This question arises in different ways in different parts of the world. In the rich and developed countries there is a disturbing decline or collapse of the birthrate. The poorer countries, on the other hand, generally have a high rate of population growth, difficult to sustain in the context of low economic and social development, and especially where there is extreme underdevelopment. In the face of over-

population in the poorer countries, instead of forms of global intervention at the international level—serious family and social policies, programmes of cultural development and of fair production and distribution of resources—anti-birth policies continue to be enacted.

Contraception, sterilization and abortion are certainly part of the reason why in some cases there is a sharp decline in the birthrate. It is not difficult to be tempted to use the same methods and attacks against life also where there is a situation of "demographic explosion".

The Pharaoh of old, haunted by the presence and increase of the children of Israel, submitted them to every kind of oppression and ordered that every male child born of the Hebrew women was to be killed (cf. *Ex* 1:7-22). Today not a few of the powerful of the earth act in the same way. They too are haunted by the current demographic growth, and fear that the most prolific and poorest peoples represent a threat for the well-being and peace of their own countries. Consequently, rather than wishing to face and solve these serious problems with respect for the dignity of individuals and families and for every person's inviolable right to life, they prefer to promote and impose by whatever means a massive programme of birth control. Even the economic help which they would be ready to give is unjustly made conditional on the acceptance of an anti-birth policy.

17.   Humanity today offers us a truly alarming spectacle, if we consider not only how extensively attacks on life are spreading but also their unheard-of numerical proportion, and the fact that they receive widespread and powerful support from a broad consensus on the part of society, from widespread legal approval and the involvement of certain sectors of health-care personnel.

As I emphatically stated at Denver, on the occasion of the Eighth World Youth Day, "with time the threats against life have not grown weaker. They are taking on vast proportions. They are not only threats coming from the outside, from the forces of nature or the 'Cains' who kill the 'Abels'; no, they are *scientifically and systematically programmed threats*. The twentieth century will have been an era of massive attacks on life, an endless series of wars and a continual taking of innocent human life. False prophets and false teachers have had the greatest success".[15] Aside from intentions, which can be varied and perhaps can seem convincing at times, especially if presented in the name of solidarity, we are in fact faced by an objective *"conspiracy against life"*, involving even international Institutions, engaged in encouraging and carrying out actual campaigns to make contraception, sterilization and abortion widely available. Nor can it be denied that the mass media are often implicated in this conspiracy, by lending credit to that culture which presents recourse to contraception, sterilization, abortion and even euthanasia as a mark of progress and a victory of freedom, while depicting as enemies of freedom and progress those positions which are unreservedly pro-life.

"Am I my brother's keeper?" (*Gen* 4:9): *a perverse idea of freedom*

18.   The panorama described needs to be understood not only in terms of the phenomena of death which characterize it but also in the *variety of causes* which determine it. The Lord's question: "What have you done?" (*Gen* 4:10), seems almost like an invitation addressed to Cain to go beyond the material dimension of his murderous gesture, in order to recognize in it all the gravity of the *motives* which occasioned it and the *consequences* which result from it.

Decisions that go against life sometimes arise

from difficult or even tragic situations of profound suffering, loneliness, a total lack of economic prospects, depression and anxiety about the future. Such circumstances can mitigate even to a notable degree subjective responsibility and the consequent culpability of those who make these choices which in themselves are evil. But today the problem goes far beyond the necessary recognition of these personal situations. It is a problem which exists at the cultural, social and political level, where it reveals its more sinister and disturbing aspect in the tendency, ever more widely shared, to interpret the above crimes against life as *legitimate expressions of individual freedom, to be acknowledged and protected as actual rights.*

In this way, and with tragic consequences, a long historical process is reaching a turning-point. The process which once led to discovering the idea of "human rights"—rights inherent in every person and prior to any Constitution and State legislation—is today marked by a *surprising contradiction.* Precisely in an age when the inviolable rights of the person are solemnly proclaimed and the value of life is publicly affirmed, the very right to life is being denied or trampled upon, especially at the more significant moments of existence: the moment of birth and the moment of death.

On the one hand, the various declarations of human rights and the many initiatives inspired by these declarations show that at the global level there is a growing moral sensitivity, more alert to acknowledging the value and dignity of every individual as a human being, without any distinction of race, nationality, religion, political opinion or social class.

On the other hand, these noble proclamations are unfortunately contradicted by a tragic repudiation of them in practice. This denial is still more distressing, indeed more scandalous, precisely because it is occurring in a society which makes the affirmation and protection of human rights its primary objective and its boast. How can these repeated affirmations of principle be reconciled with the continual increase and widespread justification of attacks on human life? How can we reconcile these declarations with the refusal to accept those who are weak and needy, or elderly, or those who have just been conceived? These attacks go directly against respect for life and they represent a *direct threat to the entire culture of human rights*. It is a threat capable, in the end, of jeopardizing the very meaning of democratic coexistence: *rather than societies of "people living together", our cities risk becoming societies of people who are rejected,* marginalized, uprooted and oppressed. If we then look at the wider worldwide perspective, how can we fail to think that the very affirmation of the rights of individuals and peoples made in distinguished international assemblies is a merely futile exercise of rhetoric, if we fail to unmask the selfishness of the rich countries which exclude poorer countries from access to development or make such access dependent on arbitrary prohibitions against pro-creation, setting up an opposition between devel-opment and man himself? Should we not question the very economic models often adopted by States which, also as a result of international pres-sures and forms of conditioning, cause and aggra-vate situations of injustice and violence in which the life of whole peoples is degraded and trampled upon?

19.   What are *the roots of this remarkable con-tradiction?*

We can find them in an overall assessment of a cultural and moral nature, beginning with the mentality which *carries the concept of subjectiv-ity to an extreme* and even distorts it, and recog-nizes as a subject of rights only the person who enjoys full or at least incipient autonomy and who emerges from a state of total dependence on oth-ers. But how can we reconcile this approach with *the exaltation of man as a being who is "not to be used"?* The theory of human rights is based precisely on the affirmation that the human person, unlike animals and things, cannot be subjected to domination by others. We must also mention the mentality which tends to *equate personal dignity with the capacity for verbal and explicit,* or at least perceptible, *communication.* It is clear that on the basis of these presuppositions there is no place in the world for anyone who, like the unborn or the dying, is a weak element in the social structure, or for anyone who appears completely at the mercy of others and radically dependent on them, and can only communicate through the silent language of a profound sharing of affection. In this case it is force which becomes the criterion for choice and action in interpersonal relations and in social life. But this is the exact opposite of what a State ruled by law, as a community in which the "reasons of force" are replaced by the "force of reason", historically intended to affirm.

At another level, the roots of the contradiction between the solemn affirmation of human rights and their tragic denial in practice lies in a *notion of freedom* which exalts the isolated individual in an absolute way, and gives no place to solidarity, to openness to others and service of them. While it is true that the taking of life not yet born or in its final stages is sometimes marked by a mistaken sense of altruism and human compassion, it cannot be denied that such a culture of death, taken as a whole, betrays a completely individualistic concept of freedom, which ends up by becoming the freedom of "the strong" against the weak who have no choice but to submit.

It is precisely in this sense that Cain's answer to the Lord's question: "Where is Abel your brother?" can be interpreted: "I do not know; *am I my brother's keeper?*" (*Gen* 4:9). Yes, every man is his "brother's keeper", because God entrusts us to one another. And it is also in view of this entrusting that God gives everyone freedom, a freedom which possesses an *inherently relational dimension*. This is a great gift of the Creator, placed as it is at the service of the person and of his fulfilment through the gift of self and openness to others; but when freedom is made absolute in an individualistic way, it is emptied of its original content, and its very meaning and dignity are contradicted.

There is an even more profound aspect which needs to be emphasized: freedom negates and destroys itself, and becomes a factor leading to the destruction of others, when it no longer recognizes and respects *its essential link with the truth*. When freedom, out of a desire to emancipate itself from all forms of tradition and authority, shuts out even the most obvious evidence of an objective and universal truth, which is the foundation of personal and social life, then the person ends up by no longer taking as the sole and indisputable point of reference for his own choices the truth about good and evil, but only his subjective and changeable opinion or, indeed, his selfish interest and whim.

20.   This view of freedom *leads to a serious distortion of life in society*. If the promotion of the self is understood in terms of absolute autonomy, people inevitably reach the point of rejecting one another. Everyone else is considered an enemy from whom one has to defend oneself. Thus society becomes a mass of individuals placed side by side, but without any mutual bonds. Each one wishes to assert himself independently of the other and in fact intends to make his own interests prevail. Still, in the face of other people's analogous interests, some kind of compromise must be found, if one wants a society in which the maximum possible freedom is guaranteed to each individual. In this way, any reference to common values and to a truth absolutely binding on everyone is lost, and social life ventures on to the shift-

41

ing sands of complete relativism. At that point, *everything is negotiable, everything is open to bargaining:* even the first of the fundamental rights, the right to life.

This is what is happening also at the level of politics and government: the original and inalienable right to life is questioned or denied on the basis of a parliamentary vote or the will of one part of the people—even if it is the majority. This is the sinister result of a relativism which reigns unopposed: the "right" ceases to be such, because it is no longer firmly founded on the inviolable dignity of the person, but is made subject to the will of the stronger part. In this way democracy, contradicting its own principles, effectively moves towards a form of totalitarianism. The State is no longer the "common home" where all can live together on the basis of principles of fundamental equality, but is transformed into a *tyrant State,* which arrogates to itself the right to dispose of the life of the weakest and most defenceless members, from the unborn child to the elderly, in the name of a public interest which is really nothing but the interest of one part. The appearance of the strictest respect for legality is maintained, at least when the laws permitting abortion and euthanasia are the result of a ballot in accordance with what are generally seen as the rules of democracy. Really, what we have here is only the tragic caricature of legality; the democratic ideal, which is only truly such when it acknowledges and safeguards the dignity of every human person, *is betrayed in its very foundations:* "How is it still possible to speak of the dignity of every human person when the killing of the weakest and most innocent is permitted? In the name of what justice is the most unjust of discriminations practised: some individuals are held to be deserving of defence and others are denied that dignity?" [16] When this happens, the process leading to the breakdown of a genuinely human coexistence and the disintegration of the State itself has already begun.

To claim the right to abortion, infanticide and euthanasia, and to recognize that right in law, means to attribute to human freedom a *perverse and evil significance:* that of an *absolute power over others and against others*. This is the death of true freedom: "Truly, truly, I say to you, every one who commits sin is a slave to sin" (*Jn* 8:34).

"And from your face I shall be hidden" (*Gen* 4:14): *the eclipse of the sense of God and of man*

21. In seeking the deepest roots of the struggle between the "culture of life" and the "culture of death", we cannot restrict ourselves to the perverse idea of freedom mentioned above. We have to go to the heart of the tragedy being experienced by modern man: *the eclipse of the sense of God and of man,* typical of a social and cultural climate dominated by secularism, which, with its ubiquitous tentacles, succeeds at times in putting Christian communities themselves to the test. Those who allow themselves to be influenced by this climate easily fall into a sad vicious circle: *when the sense of God is lost, there is also a tendency to lose the sense of man,* of his dignity and his life; in turn, the systematic violation of the moral law, especially in the serious matter of respect for human life and its dignity, produces a kind of progressive darkening of the capacity to discern God's living and saving presence.

Once again we can gain insight from the story of Abel's murder by his brother. After the curse imposed on him by God, Cain thus addresses the Lord: "My punishment is greater than I can bear. Behold, you have driven me this day away from the ground; and *from your face I shall be hidden;*

and I shall be a fugitive and wanderer on the earth, and whoever finds me will slay me" (*Gen* 4:13-14). Cain is convinced that his sin will not obtain pardon from the Lord and that his inescapable destiny will be to have to "hide his face" from him. If Cain is capable of confessing that his fault is "greater than he can bear", it is because he is conscious of being in the presence of God and before God's just judgment. It is really only before the Lord that man can admit his sin and recognize its full seriousness. Such was the experience of David who, after "having committed evil in the sight of the Lord", and being rebuked by the Prophet Nathan, exclaimed: "My offences truly I know them; my sin is always before me. Against you, you alone, have I sinned; what is evil in your sight I have done" (*Ps* 51:5-6).

22.   Consequently, when the sense of God is lost, the sense of man is also threatened and poisoned, as the Second Vatican Council concisely states: "Without the Creator the creature would disappear . . . But when God is forgotten the creature itself grows unintelligible".[17] Man is no longer able to see himself as "mysteriously different" from other earthly creatures; he regards himself merely as one more living being, as an organism which, at most, has reached a very high

stage of perfection. Enclosed in the narrow horizon of his physical nature, he is somehow reduced to being "a thing", and no longer grasps the "transcendent" character of his "existence as man". He no longer considers life as a splendid gift of God, something "sacred" entrusted to his responsibility and thus also to his loving care and "veneration". Life itself becomes a mere "thing", which man claims as his exclusive property, completely subject to his control and manipulation.

Thus, in relation to life at birth or at death, man is no longer capable of posing the question of the truest meaning of his own existence, nor can he assimilate with genuine freedom these crucial moments of his own history. He is concerned only with "doing", and, using all kinds of technology, he busies himself with programming, controlling and dominating birth and death. Birth and death, instead of being primary experiences demanding to be "lived", become things to be merely "possessed" or "rejected".

Moreover, once all reference to God has been removed, it is not surprising that the meaning of everything else becomes profoundly distorted. Nature itself, from being *"mater"* (mother), is now reduced to being "matter", and is subjected to every kind of manipulation. This is the direction in which a certain technical and scientific way of thinking, prevalent in present-day culture, appears to be leading when it rejects the very idea that there is a truth of creation which must be acknowledged, or a plan of God for life which must be respected. Something similar happens when concern about the consequences of such a "freedom without law" leads some people to the opposite position of a "law without freedom", as for example in ideologies which consider it unlawful to interfere in any way with nature, practically "divinizing" it. Again, this is a misunderstanding of nature's dependence on the plan of the Creator. Thus it is clear that the loss of contact with God's wise design is the deepest root of modern man's confusion, both when this loss leads to a freedom without rules and when it leaves man in a "fear" of his freedom.

By living "as if God did not exist", man not only loses sight of the mystery of God, but also of the mystery of the world and the mystery of his own being.

23.   The eclipse of the sense of God and of man inevitably leads to a *practical materialism*, which breeds individualism, utilitarianism and hedonism. Here too we see the permanent validity

of the words of the Apostle: "And since they did not see fit to acknowledge God, God gave them up to a base mind and to improper conduct" (*Rom* 1:28). The values of *being* are replaced by those of *having*. The only goal which counts is the pursuit of one's own material well-being. The so-called "quality of life" is interpreted primarily or exclusively as economic efficiency, inordinate consumerism, physical beauty and pleasure, to the neglect of the more profound dimensions— interpersonal, spiritual and religious—of existence.

In such a context *suffering,* an inescapable burden of human existence but also a factor of possible personal growth, is "censored", rejected as useless, indeed opposed as an evil, always and in every way to be avoided. When it cannot be avoided and the prospect of even some future well-being vanishes, then life appears to have lost all meaning and the temptation grows in man to claim the right to suppress it.

Within this same cultural climate, the *body* is no longer perceived as a properly personal reality, a sign and place of relations with others, with God and with the world. It is reduced to pure materiality: it is simply a complex of organs, functions and energies to be used according to the sole criteria of pleasure and efficiency. Consequently, *sexuality* too is depersonalized and exploited: from being the sign, place and language of love, that is, of the gift of self and acceptance of another, in all the other's richness as a person, it increasingly becomes the occasion and instrument for self-assertion and the selfish satisfaction of personal desires and instincts. Thus the original import of human sexuality is distorted and falsified, and the two meanings, unitive and procreative, inherent in the very nature of the conjugal act, are artificially separated: in this way the marriage union is betrayed and its fruitfulness is subjected to the caprice of the couple. *Procreation* then becomes the "enemy" to be avoided in sexual activity: if it is welcomed, this is only because it expresses a desire, or indeed the intention, to have a child "at all costs", and not because it signifies the complete acceptance of the other and therefore an openness to the richness of life which the child represents.

In the materialistic perspective described so far, *interpersonal relations are seriously impoverished*. The first to be harmed are women, children, the sick or suffering, and the elderly. The criterion of personal dignity—which demands respect, generosity and service—is replaced by the criterion of efficiency, functionality and usefulness: others are considered not for what they "are", but for what they "have, do and produce". This is the supremacy of the strong over the weak.

24.   *It is at the heart of the moral conscience* that the eclipse of the sense of God and of man, with all its various and deadly consequences for life, is taking place. It is a question, above all, of the *individual* conscience, as it stands before God in its singleness and uniqueness.[18] But it is also a question, in a certain sense, of the "moral conscience" *of society:* in a way it too is responsible, not only because it tolerates or fosters behaviour contrary to life, but also because it encourages the "culture of death", creating and consolidating actual "structures of sin" which go against life. The moral conscience, both individual and social, is today subjected, also as a result of the penetrating influence of the media, to an *extremely serious and mortal danger:* that of *confusion between good and evil,* precisely in relation to the fundamental right to life. A large part of contemporary society looks sadly like that humanity which Paul describes in his Letter to the Romans. It is composed "of men who by their wickedness suppress the truth" (1:18): having denied God and believing that they can build the earthly city without him, "they became futile in their thinking" so that

"their senseless minds were darkened" (1:21); "claiming to be wise, they became fools" (1:22), carrying out works deserving of death, and "they not only do them but approve those who practise them" (1:32). When conscience, this bright lamp of the soul (cf. *Mt* 6:22-23), calls "evil good and good evil" (*Is* 5:20), it is already on the path to the most alarming corruption and the darkest moral blindness.

And yet all the conditioning and efforts to enforce silence fail to stifle the voice of the Lord echoing in the conscience of every individual: it is always from this intimate sanctuary of the conscience that a new journey of love, openness and service to human life can begin.

"You have come to the sprinkled blood" (cf. *Heb* 12: 22, 24): *signs of hope and invitation to commitment*

25.   "The voice of your brother's blood is crying to me from the ground" (*Gen* 4:10). It is not only the voice of the blood of Abel, the first innocent man to be murdered, which cries to God, the source and defender of life. The blood of every other human being who has been killed since Abel is also a voice raised to the Lord. In an absolutely

singular way, as the author of the Letter to the Hebrews reminds us, *the voice of the blood of Christ,* of whom Abel in his innocence is a prophetic figure, cries out to God: "You have come to Mount Zion and to the city of the living God . . . to the mediator of a new covenant, and to the sprinkled blood that speaks more graciously than the blood of Abel" (12:22, 24).

It is *the sprinkled blood.* A symbol and prophetic sign of it had been the blood of the sacrifices of the Old Covenant, whereby God expressed his will to communicate his own life to men, purifying and consecrating them (cf. *Ex* 24:8; *Lev* 17:11). Now all of this is fulfilled and comes true in Christ: his is the sprinkled blood which redeems, purifies and saves; it is the blood of the Mediator of the New Covenant "poured out for many for the forgiveness of sins" (*Mt* 26:28). This blood, which flows from the pierced side of Christ on the Cross (cf. *Jn* 19:34), "speaks more graciously" than the blood of Abel; indeed, it expresses and requires a more radical "justice", and above all it implores mercy,[19] it makes intercession for the brethren before the Father (cf. *Heb* 7:25), and it is the source of perfect redemption and the gift of new life.

The blood of Christ, while it reveals the grandeur of the Father's love, *shows how precious man is in God's eyes and how priceless the value of his life.* The Apostle Peter reminds us of this: "You know that you were ransomed from the futile ways inherited from your fathers, not with perishable things such as silver or gold, but with the precious blood of Christ, like that of a lamb without blemish or spot" (1 *Pt* 1:18-19). Precisely by contemplating the precious blood of Christ, the sign of his self-giving love (cf. *Jn* 13:1), the believer learns to recognize and appreciate the almost divine dignity of every human being and can exclaim with ever renewed and grateful wonder: "How precious must man be in the eyes of the Creator, if he 'gained so great a Redeemer' (*Exsultet* of the Easter Vigil), and if God 'gave his only Son' in order that man should not perish but have eternal life' (cf. *Jn* 3:16)!".[20]

Furthermore, Christ's blood reveals to man that his greatness, and therefore his vocation, consists in *the sincere gift of self.* Precisely because it is poured out as the gift of life, the blood of Christ is no longer a sign of death, of definitive separation from the brethren, but the instrument of a communion which is richness of life for all. Whoever in the Sacrament of the Eucharist drinks this blood and abides in Jesus (cf. *Jn* 6:56) is drawn into the dynamism of his love and gift of life, in order to bring to its fullness the original vocation to love which belongs to everyone (cf. *Gen* 1:27; 2:18-24).

It is from the blood of Christ that all draw *the strength to commit themselves to promoting life.* It is precisely this blood that is *the most powerful source of hope, indeed it is the foundation of the absolute certitude that in God's plan life will be victorious.* "And death shall be no more", exclaims the powerful voice which comes from the throne of God in the Heavenly Jerusalem (*Rev* 21:4). And Saint Paul assures us that the present victory over sin is a sign and anticipation of the definitive victory over death, when there "shall come to pass the saying that is written: 'Death is swallowed up in victory'. 'O death, where is your victory? O death, where is your sting?' " (1 *Cor* 15:54-55).

26.   In effect, signs which point to this victory are not lacking in our societies and cultures, strongly marked though they are by the "culture of death". It would therefore be to give a one-sided picture, which could lead to sterile discouragement, if the condemnation of the threats to life were not accompanied by the presentation of the *positive signs* at work in humanity's present situation.

Unfortunately it is often hard to see and recognize these positive signs, perhaps also because they do not receive sufficient attention in the communications media. Yet, how many initiatives of help and support for people who are weak and defenceless have sprung up and continue to spring up in the Christian community and in civil society, at the local, national and international level, through the efforts of individuals, groups, movements and organizations of various kinds!

There are still many *married couples* who, with a generous sense of responsibility, are ready to accept children as "the supreme gift of marriage".[21] Nor is there a lack of *families* which, over and above their everyday service to life, are willing to accept abandoned children, boys and girls and teenagers in difficulty, handicapped persons, elderly men and women who have been left alone. Many *centres in support of life,* or similar institutions, are sponsored by individuals and groups which, with admirable dedication and sacrifice, offer moral and material support to mothers who are in difficulty and are tempted to have recourse to abortion. Increasingly, there are appearing in many places *groups of volunteers* prepared to offer hospitality to persons without a family, who find themselves in conditions of particular distress or who need a supportive environment to help them to overcome destructive habits and discover anew the meaning of life.

Medical science, thanks to the committed efforts of researchers and practitioners, continues in its efforts to discover ever more effective remedies: treatments which were once inconceivable but which now offer much promise for the future are today being developed for the unborn, the suffering and those in an acute or terminal stage of sickness. Various agencies and organizations are mobilizing their efforts to bring the benefits of the most advanced medicine to countries most afflicted by poverty and endemic diseases. In a similar way national and international associations of physicians are being organized to bring quick relief to peoples affected by natural disasters, epidemics or wars. Even if a just international distribution of medical resources is still far from being a reality, how can we not recognize in the steps taken so far the sign of a growing solidarity among peoples, a praiseworthy human and moral sensitivity and a greater respect for life?

27.   In view of laws which permit abortion and in view of efforts, which here and there have been successful, to legalize euthanasia, *movements and initiatives to raise social awareness in de-*

fence of life have sprung up in many parts of the world. When, in accordance with their principles, such movements act resolutely, but without resorting to violence, they promote a wider and more profound consciousness of the value of life, and evoke and bring about a more determined commitment to its defence.

Furthermore, how can we fail to mention *all those daily gestures of openness, sacrifice and unselfish care* which countless people lovingly make in families, hospitals, orphanages, homes for the elderly and other centres or communities which defend life? Allowing herself to be guided by the example of Jesus the "Good Samaritan" (cf. *Lk* 10:29-37) and upheld by his strength, the Church has always been in the front line in providing charitable help: so many of her sons and daughters, especially men and women Religious, in traditional and ever new forms, have consecrated and continue to consecrate their lives to God, freely giving of themselves out of love for their neighbour, especially for the weak and needy. These deeds strengthen the bases of the "civilization of love and life", without which the life of individuals and of society itself loses its most genuinely human quality. Even if they go unnoticed and remain hidden to most people, faith assures us that the Father "who sees in secret" (*Mt* 6:6) not only will reward these actions but already here and now makes them produce lasting fruit for the good of all.

Among the signs of hope we should also count the spread, at many levels of public opinion, of *a new sensitivity ever more opposed to war* as an instrument for the resolution of conflicts between peoples, and increasingly oriented to finding effective but "non-violent" means to counter the armed aggressor. In the same perspective there is evidence of a *growing public opposition to the death penalty,* even when such a penalty is seen as a kind of "legitimate defence" on the part of society. Modern society in fact has the means of effectively suppressing crime by rendering criminals harmless without definitively denying them the chance to reform.

Another welcome sign is the growing attention being paid to the *quality of life* and to *ecology,* especially in more developed societies, where people's expectations are no longer concentrated so much on problems of survival as on the search for an overall improvement of living conditions. Especially significant is the reawakening of an ethical reflection on issues affecting life. The emergence and ever more widespread development of *bioethics* is promoting more reflection and dialogue—between believers and non-believers, as well as between followers of different religions—on ethical problems, including fundamental issues pertaining to human life.

28.   This situation, with its lights and shadows, ought to make us all fully aware that we are facing an enormous and dramatic clash between good and evil, death and life, the "culture of death" and the "culture of life". We find ourselves not only "faced with" but necessarily "in the midst of" this conflict: we are all involved and we all share in it, with the inescapable responsibility of *choosing to be unconditionally pro-life*.

For us too Moses' invitation rings out loud and clear: "See, I have set before you this day life and good, death and evil. . . . I have set before you life and death, blessing and curse; *therefore choose life, that you and your descendants may live*" (*Dt* 30:15, 19). This invitation is very appropriate for us who are called day by day to the duty of choosing between the "culture of life" and the "culture of death". But the call of Deuteronomy goes even deeper, for it urges us to make a choice which is properly religious and moral. It is a question of giving our own existence a basic orientation and living the law of the Lord faithfully and consistently: "If you obey the commandments of the Lord your God which I command you this day, by *loving the Lord your God,* by *walking in his ways,* and by *keeping his commandments* and his statutes and his ordinances, then you shall live . . . therefore choose life, that you and your descendants may live, loving the Lord your God, obeying his voice, and cleaving to him; *for that means life to you and length of days"* (30:16,19-20).

The unconditional choice for life reaches its full religious and moral meaning when it flows from, is formed by and nourished by *faith in Christ.* Nothing helps us so much to face positively the conflict between death and life in which we are engaged as faith in the Son of God who became man and dwelt among men so "that they may have life, and have it abundantly" (*Jn* 10:10). It is a matter of *faith in the Risen Lord, who has conquered death;* faith in the blood of Christ "that speaks more graciously than the blood of Abel" (*Heb* 12:24).

With the light and strength of this faith, therefore, in facing the challenges of the present situation, the Church is becoming more aware of the grace and responsibility which come to her from her Lord of proclaiming, celebrating and serving the *Gospel of life.*

CHAPTER II
I CAME
THAT THEY MAY HAVE LIFE

THE CHRISTIAN MESSAGE CONCERNING LIFE

"The life was made manifest, and we saw it" (*1 Jn* 1:2): *with our gaze fixed on Christ, "the Word of life"*

29.   Faced with the countless grave threats to life present in the modern world, one could feel overwhelmed by sheer powerlessness: good can never be powerful enough to triumph over evil!

At such times the People of God, and this includes every believer, is called to profess with humility and courage its faith in Jesus Christ, "the Word of life" (1 *Jn* 1:1). The *Gospel of life* is not simply a reflection, however new and profound, on human life. Nor is it merely a commandment aimed at raising awareness and bringing about significant changes in society. Still less is it an illusory promise of a better future. The *Gospel of life* is something concrete and personal, for it consists in the proclamation of *the very person of Jesus.*

Jesus made himself known to the Apostle Thomas, and in him to every person, with the words: "I am the way, and the truth, and the life" (*Jn* 14:6). This is also how he spoke of himself to Martha, the sister of Lazarus: "I am the resurrection and the life; he who believes in me, though he die, yet shall he live, and whoever lives and believes in me shall never die" (*Jn* 11:25-26). Jesus is the Son who from all eternity receives life from the Father (cf. *Jn* 5:26), and who has come among men to make them sharers in this gift: "I came that they may have life, and have it abundantly" (*Jn* 10:10).

Through the words, the actions and the very person of Jesus, man is given the possibility of "knowing" *the complete truth* concerning the value of human life. From this "source" he receives, in particular, the capacity to "accomplish" this truth perfectly (cf. *Jn* 3:21), that is, to accept and fulfil completely the responsibility of loving and serving, of defending and promoting human life. In Christ, the *Gospel of life* is definitively proclaimed and fully given. This is the Gospel which, already present in the Revelation of the Old Testament, and indeed written in the heart of every man and woman, has echoed in every conscience "from the beginning", from the time of creation itself, in such a way that, despite the negative consequences of sin, *it can also be known in its essential traits by human reason.* As the Second Vatican Council teaches, Christ "perfected revelation by fulfilling it through his whole work of making himself present and manifesting himself; through his words and deeds, his signs and wonders, but especially through his death and glorious Resurrection from the dead and final sending of the Spirit of truth. Moreover, he confirmed with divine testimony what revelation proclaimed: that God is with us to free us from the darkness of sin and death, and to raise us up to life eternal".[22]

30.   Hence, with our attention fixed on the Lord Jesus, we wish to hear from him once again "the words of God" (*Jn* 3:34) and meditate anew on the *Gospel of life.* The deepest and most original meaning of this meditation on what revelation tells us about human life was taken up by the Apostle John in the opening words of his First Letter: "That which was from the beginning, which we have heard, which we have seen with our eyes, which we have looked upon and touched with our hands, concerning the word of life—the life was made manifest, and we saw it, and testify to it, and proclaim to you the eternal life which was with the Father and was made

manifest to us—that which we have seen and heard we proclaim also to you, so that you may have fellowship with us" (1:1-3).

In Jesus, the "Word of life", God's eternal life is thus proclaimed and given. Thanks to this proclamation and gift, our physical and spiritual life, also in its earthly phase, acquires its full value and meaning, for God's eternal life is in fact the end to which our living in this world is directed and called. In this way the *Gospel of life* includes everything that human experience and reason tell us about the value of human life, accepting it, purifying it, exalting it and bringing it to fulfilment.

"The Lord is my strength and my song, and he has become my salvation" (Ex 15:2): life is always a good

31.   The fullness of the Gospel message about life was prepared for in the Old Testament. Especially in the events of the Exodus, the centre of the Old Testament faith experience, Israel discovered the preciousness of its life in the eyes of God. When it seemed doomed to extermination because of the threat of death hanging over all its newborn males (cf. *Ex* 1:15-22), the Lord revealed

himself to Israel as its Saviour, with the power to ensure a future to those without hope. Israel thus comes to know clearly that *its existence* is not at the mercy of a Pharaoh who can exploit it at his despotic whim. On the contrary, Israel's life is *the object of God's gentle and intense love.*

Freedom from slavery meant the gift of an identity, the recognition of an indestructible dignity and *the beginning of a new history,* in which the discovery of God and discovery of self go hand in hand. The Exodus was a foundational experience and a model for the future. Through it, Israel comes to learn that whenever its existence is threatened it need only turn to God with renewed trust in order to find in him effective help: "I formed you, you are my servant; O Israel, you will not be forgotten by me" (*Is* 44:21).

Thus, in coming to know the value of its own existence as a people, Israel also grows in its *perception of the meaning and value of life itself.* This reflection is developed more specifically in the Wisdom Literature, on the basis of daily experience of the precariousness of life and awareness of the threats which assail it. Faced with the contradictions of life, faith is challenged to respond.

More than anything else, it is the problem of suffering which challenges faith and puts it to the test. How can we fail to appreciate the universal anguish of man when we meditate on the Book of Job? The innocent man overwhelmed by suffering is understandably led to wonder: "Why is light given to him that is in misery, and life to the bitter in soul, who long for death, but it comes not, and dig for it more than for hid treasures?" (3:20-21). But even when the darkness is deepest, faith points to a trusting and adoring acknowledgment of the "mystery": "I know that you can do all things, and that no purpose of yours can be thwarted" (*Job* 42:2).

Revelation progressively allows the first notion of immortal life planted by the Creator in the human heart to be grasped with ever greater clarity: "He has made everything beautiful in its time; also he has put eternity into man's mind" (*Ec* 3 :11). This *first notion of totality and fullness* is waiting to be manifested in love and brought to perfection, by God's free gift, through sharing in his eternal life.

"The name of Jesus . . . has made this man strong" (Acts 3:16): in the uncertainties of human life, Jesus brings life's meaning to fulfilment

32.   The experience of the people of the Covenant is renewed in the experience of all the

"poor" who meet Jesus of Nazareth. Just as God who "loves the living" (cf. *Wis* 11:26) had reassured Israel in the midst of danger, so now the Son of God proclaims to all who feel threatened and hindered that their lives too are a good to which the Father's love gives meaning and value.

"The blind receive their sight, the lame walk, lepers are cleansed, and the deaf hear, the dead are raised up, the poor have good news preached to them" (*Lk* 7:22). With these words of the Prophet Isaiah (35:5-6, 61:1), Jesus sets forth the meaning of his own mission: all who suffer because their lives are in some way "diminished" thus hear from him the "good news" of God's concern for them, and they know for certain that their lives too are a gift carefully guarded in the hands of the Father (cf. *Mt* 6:25-34).

It is above all the "poor" to whom Jesus speaks in his preaching and actions. The crowds of the sick and the outcasts who follow him and seek him out (cf. *Mt* 4:23-25) find in his words and actions a revelation of the great value of their lives and of how their hope of salvation is well-founded.

The same thing has taken place in the Church's mission from the beginning. When the Church proclaims Christ as the one who "went about doing good and healing all that were oppressed by the devil, for God was with him" (*Acts* 10:38), she is conscious of being the bearer of a message of salvation which resounds in all its newness precisely amid the hardships and poverty of human life. Peter cured the cripple who daily sought alms at the "Beautiful Gate" of the Temple in Jerusalem, saying: "I have no silver and gold, but I give you what I have; in the name of Jesus Christ of Nazareth, walk" (*Acts* 3:6). By faith in Jesus, "the Author of life" (*Acts* 3:15), life which lies abandoned and cries out for help regains self-esteem and full dignity.

The words and deeds of Jesus and those of his Church are not meant only for those who are sick or suffering or in some way neglected by society. On a deeper level they affect *the very meaning of every person's life in its moral and spiritual dimensions*. Only those who recognize that their life is marked by the evil of sin can discover in an encounter with Jesus the Saviour the truth and the authenticity of their own existence. Jesus himself says as much: "Those who are well have no need of a physician, but those who are sick; I have not come to call the righteous, but sinners to repentance" (*Lk* 5:31-32).

But the person who, like the rich land-owner in the Gospel parable, thinks that he can make his life secure by the possession of material goods alone, is deluding himself. Life is slipping away from him, and very soon he will find himself bereft of it without ever having appreciated its real meaning: "Fool! This night your soul is required of you; and the things you have prepared, whose will they be?" (*Lk* 12:20).

33.   In Jesus' own life, from beginning to end, we find a singular "dialectic" between the experience of the uncertainty of human life and the affirmation of its value. Jesus' life is marked by uncertainty from the very moment of his birth. He is certainly *accepted* by the righteous, who echo Mary's immediate and joyful "yes" (cf. *Lk* 1:38). But there is also, from the start, *rejection* on the part of a world which grows hostile and looks for the child in order "to destroy him" (*Mt* 2:13); a world which remains indifferent and unconcerned about the fulfilment of the mystery of this life entering the world: "there was no place for them in the inn" (*Lk* 2:7). In this contrast between threats and insecurity on the one hand and the power of God's gift on the other, there shines forth all the more clearly the glory which radiates from the house at Nazareth and from the manger at Bethlehem: this life which is born is salvation for all humanity (cf. *Lk* 2:11).

Life's contradictions and risks were fully accepted by Jesus: "though he was rich, yet for your sake he became poor, so that by his poverty you might become rich" (*2 Cor* 8:9). The poverty of which Paul speaks is not only a stripping of divine privileges, but also a sharing in the lowliest and most vulnerable conditions of human life (cf. *Phil* 2:6-7). Jesus lived this poverty throughout his life, until the culminating moment of the Cross: "he humbled himself and became obedient unto death, even death on a cross. Therefore God has highly exalted him and bestowed on him the name which is above every name" (*Phil* 2:8-9). It is precisely *by his death* that *Jesus reveals all the splendour and value of life,* inasmuch as his self-oblation on the Cross becomes the source of new life for all people (cf. *Jn* 12:32). In his journeying amid contradictions and in the very loss of his life, Jesus is guided by the certainty that his life is in the hands of the Father. Consequently, on the Cross, he can say to him: "Father, into your hands I commend my spirit!" (*Lk* 23:46), that is, my life. Truly great must be the value of human life if the Son of God has taken it up and made it the instrument of the salvation of all humanity!

*"Called . . . to be conformed to the image of his
Son" (Rom 8:28-29): God's glory shines on the
face of man*

34.   Life is always a good. This is an instinc-
tive perception and a fact of experience, and man
is called to grasp the profound reason why this
is so.

Why is life a good? This question is found
everywhere in the Bible, and from the very first
pages it receives a powerful and amazing answer.
The life which God gives man is quite different
from the life of all other living creatures, inasmuch as man, although formed from the dust of
the earth (cf. *Gen* 2:7, 3:19; *Job* 34:15; *Ps* 103:14;
104:29), *is a manifestation of God in the world, a
sign of his presence, a trace of his glory* (cf. *Gen*
1:26-27; *Ps* 8:6). This is what Saint Irenaeus of
Lyons wanted to emphasize in his celebrated
definition: "Man, living man, is the glory of
God".[23] Man has been given *a sublime dignity,*
based on the intimate bond which unites him to
his Creator: in man there shines forth a reflection
of God himself.

The Book of Genesis affirms this when, in
the first account of creation, it places man at the
summit of God's creative activity, as its crown,
at the culmination of a process which leads from

indistinct chaos to the most perfect of creatures. *Everything in creation is ordered to man and everything is made subject to him:* "Fill the earth and subdue it; and have dominion over . . . every living thing" (1:28); this is God's command to the man and the woman. A similar message is found also in the other account of creation: "The Lord God took the man and put him in the garden of Eden to till it and keep it" (*Gen* 2:15). We see here a clear affirmation of the primacy of man over things; these are made subject to him and entrusted to his responsible care, whereas for no reason can he be made subject to other men and almost reduced to the level of a thing.

In the biblical narrative, the difference between man and other creatures is shown above all by the fact that only the creation of man is presented as the result of a special decision on the part of God, a deliberation to establish *a particular and specific bond with the Creator:* "Let us make man in our image, after our likeness" (*Gen* 1:26). *The life* which God offers to man *is a gift by which God shares something of himself with his creature.*

Israel would ponder at length the meaning of this particular bond between man and God. The Book of Sirach too recognizes that God, in creating human beings, "endowed them with strength like his own, and made them in his own image" (17:3). The biblical author sees as part of this image not only man's dominion over the world but also *those spiritual faculties which are distinctively human,* such as reason, discernment between good and evil, and free will: "He filled them with knowledge and understanding, and showed them good and evil" (*Sir* 17:7). *The ability to attain truth and freedom are human prerogatives* inasmuch as man is created in the image of his Creator, God who is true and just (cf. *Dt* 32:4). Man alone, among all visible creatures, is "capable of knowing and loving his Creator".[24] The life which God bestows upon man is much more than mere existence in time. It is a drive towards fullness of life; *it is the seed of an existence which transcends the very limits of time:* "For God created man for incorruption, and made him in the image of his own eternity" (*Wis* 2:23).

35.   The Yahwist account of creation expresses the same conviction. This ancient narrative speaks of *a divine breath* which *is breathed into man* so that he may come to life: "The Lord God formed man of dust from the ground, and breathed into his nostrils the breath of life; and man became a living being" (*Gen* 2:7).

The divine origin of this spirit of life explains

the perennial dissatisfaction which man feels throughout his days on earth. Because he is made by God and bears within himself an indelible imprint of God, man is naturally drawn to God. When he heeds the deepest yearnings of the heart, every man must make his own the words of truth expressed by Saint Augustine: "You have made us for yourself, O Lord, and our hearts are restless until they rest in you".[25]

How very significant is the dissatisfaction which marks man's life in Eden as long as his sole point of reference is the world of plants and animals (cf. *Gen* 2:20). Only the appearance of the woman, a being who is flesh of his flesh and bone of his bones (cf. *Gen* 2:23), and in whom the spirit of God the Creator is also alive, can satisfy the need for interpersonal dialogue, so vital for human existence. In the other, whether man or woman, there is a reflection of God himself, the definitive goal and fulfilment of every person.

"What is man that you are mindful of him, and the son of man that you care for him?", the Psalmist wonders (*Ps* 8:4). Compared to the immensity of the universe, man is very small, and yet this very contrast reveals his greatness: "You have made him little less than a god, and crown him with glory and honour" (*Ps* 8:5). *The glory of God shines on the face of man.* In man the Creator finds his rest, as Saint Ambrose comments with a sense of awe: "The sixth day is finished and the creation of the world ends with the formation of that masterpiece which is man, who exercises dominion over all living creatures and is as it were the crown of the universe and the supreme beauty of every created being. Truly we should maintain a reverential silence, since the Lord rested from every work he had undertaken in the world. He rested then in the depths of man, he rested in man's mind and in his thought; after all, he had created man endowed with reason, capable of imitating him, of emulating his virtue, of hungering for heavenly graces. In these his gifts God reposes, who has said: 'Upon whom shall I rest, if not upon the one who is humble, contrite in spirit and trembles at my word?' (*Is* 66:1-2). I thank the Lord our God who has created so wonderful a work in which to take his rest".[26]

36.   Unfortunately, God's marvellous plan was marred by the appearance of sin in history. Through sin, man rebels against his Creator and ends up by *worshipping creatures:* "They exchanged the truth about God for a lie and worshipped and served the creature rather than the Creator" (*Rom* 1:25). As a result man not only deforms the image of God in his own person, but

is tempted to offences against it in others as well, replacing relationships of communion by attitudes of distrust, indifference, hostility and even murderous hatred. When *God* is not acknowledged *as God,* the profound meaning of man is betrayed and communion between people is compromised.

In the life of man, God's image shines forth anew and is again revealed in all its fullness at the coming of the Son of God in human flesh. "Christ is the image of the invisible God" (*Col* 1:15), he "reflects the glory of God and bears the very stamp of his nature" (*Heb* 1:3). He is the perfect image of the Father.

The plan of life given to the first Adam finds at last its fulfilment in Christ. Whereas the disobedience of Adam had ruined and marred God's plan for human life and introduced death into the world, the redemptive obedience of Christ is the source of grace poured out upon the human race, opening wide to everyone the gates of the kingdom of life (cf. *Rom* 5:12-21). As the Apostle Paul states: "The first man Adam became a living being; the last Adam became a life-giving spirit" (*1 Cor* 15:45).

All who commit themselves to following Christ are given the fullness of life: the divine image is restored, renewed and brought to perfection in them. God's plan for human beings is this, that they should "be conformed to the image of his Son" (*Rom* 8:29). Only thus, in the splendour of this image, can man be freed from the slavery of idolatry, rebuild lost fellowship and rediscover his true identity.

"Whoever lives and believes in me shall never die" (Jn 11:26): the gift of eternal life

37.   The life which the Son of God came to give to human beings cannot be reduced to mere existence in time. The life which was always "in him" and which is the "light of men" (*Jn* 1:4) *consists in being begotten of God and sharing in the fullness of his love:* "To all who received him, who believed in his name, he gave power to become children of God; who were born, not of blood nor of the will of the flesh nor of the will of man, but of God" (*Jn* 1:12-13).

Sometimes Jesus refers to this life which he came to give simply as "life", and he presents being born of God as a necessary condition if man is to attain the end for which God has created him: "Unless one is born anew, he cannot see the kingdom of God" (*Jn* 3:3). To give this life is the real object of Jesus' mission: he is the one who "comes down from heaven, and gives life to the world" (*Jn* 6:33). Thus can he truly say: "He who follows me . . . will have the light of life" (*Jn* 8:12).

At other times, Jesus speaks of "eternal life". Here the adjective does more than merely evoke a perspective which is beyond time. The life which Jesus promises and gives is "eternal" because it is a full participation in the life of the "Eternal One". Whoever believes in Jesus and enters into communion with him has eternal life (cf. *Jn* 3:15; 6:40) because he hears from Jesus the only words which reveal and communicate to his existence the fullness of life. These are the "words of eternal life" which Peter acknowledges in his confession of faith: "Lord, to whom shall we go? You have the words of eternal life; and we have believed, and have come to know, that you are the Holy One of God" (*Jn* 6:68-69). Jesus himself, addressing the Father in the great priestly prayer, declares what eternal life consists in: "This is eternal life, that they may know you the only true God, and Jesus Christ whom you have sent" (*Jn* 17:3). To know God and his Son is to accept the mystery of the loving communion of the Father, the Son and the Holy Spirit into one's own life, which *even now* is open to eternal life because it *shares in the life of God*.

38.   Eternal life is therefore the life of God himself and at the same time the *life of the children of God*. As they ponder this unexpected and inexpressible truth which comes to us from God in Christ, believers cannot fail to be filled with ever new wonder and unbounded gratitude. They can say in the words of the Apostle John: "See what love the Father has given us, that we should be called children of God; and so we are. . . . Beloved, we are God's children now; it does not yet appear what we shall be, but we know that when he appears we shall be like him, for we shall see him as he is" (*1 Jn* 3:1-2).

Here the Christian truth about life becomes most sublime. The dignity of this life is linked not only to its beginning, to the fact that it comes from God, but also to its final end, to its destiny of fellowship with God in knowledge and love of him. In the light of this truth Saint Irenaeus qualifies and completes his praise of man: "the glory of God" is indeed, "man, living man", but "the life of man consists in the vision of God".[27]

Immediate consequences arise from this for human life in its *earthly state,* in which, for that matter, eternal life already springs forth and begins to grow. Although man instinctively loves life because it is a good, this love will find further inspiration and strength, and new breadth and depth, in the divine dimensions of this good. Similarly, the love which every human being has for life cannot be reduced simply to a desire to have sufficient space for self-expression and for entering into relationships with others; rather, it develops in a joyous awareness that life can become the "place" where God manifests himself, where we meet him and enter into communion with him. The life which Jesus gives in no way lessens the value of our existence in time; it takes it and directs it to its final destiny: "I am the resurrection and the life . . . whoever lives and believes in me shall never die" (*Jn* 11:25-26).

"From man in regard to his fellow man I will demand an accounting" (Gen 9:5): reverence and love for every human life

39.   Man's life comes from God; it is his gift, his image and imprint, a sharing in his breath of life. *God* therefore *is the sole Lord of this life:* man cannot do with it as he wills. God himself makes this clear to Noah after the Flood: "For your own lifeblood, too, I will demand an accounting . . . and from man in regard to his fellow man I will demand an accounting for human

life'' (*Gen* 9:5). The biblical text is concerned to emphasize how the sacredness of life has its foundation in God and in his creative activity: ''For God made man in his own image'' (*Gen* 9:6).

Human life and death are thus in the hands of God, in his power: ''In his hand is the life of every living thing and the breath of all mankind'', exclaims Job (12:10). ''The Lord brings to death and brings to life; he brings down to Sheol and raises up'' (*1 Sam* 2:6). He alone can say: ''It is I who bring both death and life'' (*Dt* 32:39).

But God does not exercise this power in an arbitrary and threatening way, but rather as part of his *care and loving concern for his creatures.* If it is true that human life is in the hands of God, it is no less true that these are loving hands, like those of a mother who accepts, nurtures and takes care of her child: ''I have calmed and quieted my soul, like a child quieted at its mother's breast; like a child that is quieted is my soul'' (*Ps* 131:2; cf. *Is* 49:15; 66:12-13; *Hos* 11:4). Thus Israel does not see in the history of peoples and in the destiny of individuals the outcome of mere chance or of blind fate, but rather the results of a loving plan by which God brings together all the possibilities of life and opposes the powers of death arising from sin: ''God did not make death, and he does not delight in the death of the living.

81

For he created all things that they might exist"
(*Wis* 1:13-14).

40.   The sacredness of life gives rise to its *inviolability, written from the beginning in man's heart,* in his conscience. The question: "What have you done?" (*Gen* 4:10), which God addresses to Cain after he has killed his brother Abel, interprets the experience of every person: in the depths of his conscience, man is always reminded of the inviolability of life—his own life and that of others—as something which does not belong to him, because it is the property and gift of God the Creator and Father.

       The commandment regarding the inviolability of human life reverberates *at the heart of the "ten words" in the covenant of Sinai* (cf. *Ex* 34:28). In the first place that commandment prohibits murder: "You shall not kill" (*Ex* 20:13); "do not slay the innocent and righteous" (*Ex* 23:7). But, as is brought out in Israel's later legislation, it also prohibits all personal injury inflicted on another (cf. *Ex* 21:12-27). Of course we must recognize that in the Old Testament this sense of the value of life, though already quite marked, does not yet reach the refinement found in the Sermon on the Mount. This is apparent in some aspects of the current penal legislation, which

82

provided for severe forms of corporal punishment and even the death penalty. But the overall message, which the New Testament will bring to perfection, is a forceful appeal for respect for the inviolability of physical life and the integrity of the person. It culminates in the positive commandment which obliges us to be responsible for our neighbour as for ourselves: "You shall love your neighbour as yourself" (*Lev* 19:18).

41.   The commandment "You shall not kill", included and more fully expressed in the positive command of love for one's neighbour, is *reaffirmed in all its force by the Lord Jesus*. To the rich young man who asks him: "Teacher, what good deed must I do, to have eternal life?", Jesus replies: "If you would enter life, keep the commandments" (*Mt* 19:16, 17). And he quotes, as the first of these: "You shall not kill" (*Mt* 19:18). In the Sermon on the Mount, Jesus demands from his disciples a *righteousness which surpasses* that of the Scribes and Pharisees, also with regard to respect for life: "You have heard that it was said to the men of old, 'You shall not kill; and whoever kills shall be liable to judgment'. But I say to you that every one who is angry with his brother shall be liable to judgment" (*Mt* 5:21-22).

By his words and actions Jesus further unveils the positive requirements of the command-ment regarding the inviolability of life. These requirements were already present in the Old Testament, where legislation dealt with protecting and defending life when it was weak and threatened: in the case of foreigners, widows, orphans, the sick and the poor in general, including children in the womb (cf. *Ex* 21:22; 22:20-26). With Jesus these positive requirements assume new force and urgency, and are revealed in all their breadth and depth: they range from caring for the life of one's *brother* (whether a blood brother, someone belonging to the same people, or a foreigner living in the land of Israel) to showing concern for the *stranger,* even to the point of loving one's *enemy.*

A stranger is no longer a stranger for the person who must *become a neighbour* to someone in need, to the point of accepting responsibility for his life, as the parable of the Good Samaritan shows so clearly (cf. *Lk* 10:25-37). Even an enemy ceases to be an enemy for the person who is obliged to love him (cf. *Mt* 5:38-48; *Lk* 6:27-35), to "do good" to him (cf. *Lk* 6:27, 33, 35) and to respond to his immediate needs promptly and with no expectation of repayment (cf. *Lk* 6:34-35). The height of this love is to pray for one's enemy. By so doing we achieve harmony with the providential love of God: "But I say to you, love your enemies and pray for those who persecute you, so that you may be children of your Father who is in heaven, for he makes his sun rise on the evil and on the good and sends rain on the just and on the unjust" (*Mt* 5:44-45; cf. *Lk* 6:28, 35).

Thus the deepest element of God's commandment to protect human life is the *requirement to show reverence and love* for every person and the life of every person. This is the teaching which the Apostle Paul, echoing the words of Jesus, addresses to the Christians in Rome: "The commandments, 'You shall not commit adultery, You shall not kill, You shall not steal, You shall not covet', and any other commandment, are summed up in this sentence, *'You shall love your neighbour as yourself'*. Love does no wrong to a neighbour; therefore love is the fulfilling of the law" (*Rom* 13:9-10).

"Be fruitful and multiply, and fill the earth and subdue it" (Gen 1:28): man's responsibility for life

42.   To defend and promote life, to show reverence and love for it, is a task which God entrusts to every man, calling him as his living image

to share in his own lordship over the world: "God blessed them, and God said to them, 'Be fruitful and multiply, and fill the earth and subdue it; and have dominion over the fish of the sea and over the birds of the air and over every living thing that moves upon the earth' " (*Gen* 1:28).

The biblical text clearly shows the breadth and depth of the lordship which God bestows on man. It is a matter first of all of *dominion over the earth and over every living creature,* as the Book of Wisdom makes clear: "O God of my fathers and Lord of mercy . . . by your wisdom you have formed man, to have dominion over the creatures you have made, and rule the world in holiness and righteousness" (*Wis* 9:1, 2-3). The Psalmist too extols the dominion given to man as a sign of glory and honour from his Creator: "You have given him dominion over the works of your hands; you have put all things under his feet, all sheep and oxen, and also the beasts of the field, the birds of the air, and the fish of the sea, whatever passes along the paths of the sea" (*Ps* 8:6-8).

As one called to till and look after the garden of the world (cf. *Gen* 2:15), man has a specific responsibility towards *the environment in which he lives,* towards the creation which God has put at the service of his personal dignity, of his life, not only for the present but also for future generations. It is the *ecological question*—ranging from the preservation of the natural habitats of the different species of animals and of other forms of life to "human ecology" properly speaking [28]—which finds in the Bible clear and strong ethical direction, leading to a solution which respects the great good of life, of every life. In fact, "the dominion granted to man by the Creator is not an absolute power, nor can one speak of a freedom to 'use and misuse', or to dispose of things as one pleases. The limitation imposed from the beginning by the Creator himself and expressed symbolically by the prohibition not to 'eat of the fruit of the tree' (cf. *Gen* 2:16-17) shows clearly enough that, when it comes to the natural world, we are subject not only to biological laws but also to moral ones, which cannot be violated with impunity".[29]

43.   A certain sharing by man in God's lordship is also evident in the *specific responsibility* which he is given *for human life as such*. It is a responsibility which reaches its highest point in the giving of life *through procreation* by man and woman in marriage. As the Second Vatican Council teaches: "God himself who said, 'It is not good for man to be alone' (*Gen* 2:18) and 'who made man from the beginning male and female'

(*Mt* 19:4), wished to share with man a certain special participation in his own creative work. Thus he blessed male and female saying: 'Increase and multiply' (*Gen* 1:28).[30]

By speaking of "a certain special participation" of man and woman in the "creative work" of God, the Council wishes to point out that having a child is an event which is deeply human and full of religious meaning, insofar as it involves both the spouses, who form "one flesh" (*Gen* 2:24), and God who makes himself present. As I wrote in my *Letter to Families:* "When a new person is born of the conjugal union of the two, he brings with him into the world a particular image and likeness of God himself: *the genealogy of the person is inscribed in the very biology of generation.* In affirming that the spouses, as parents, cooperate with God the Creator in conceiving and giving birth to a new human being, we are not speaking merely with reference to the laws of biology. Instead, we wish to emphasize that *God himself is present in human fatherhood and motherhood* quite differently than he is present in all other instances of begetting 'on earth'. Indeed, God alone is the source of that 'image and likeness' which is proper to the human being, as it was received at Creation. Begetting is the continuation of Creation".[31]

This is what the Bible teaches in direct and eloquent language when it reports the joyful cry of the first woman, "the mother of all the living" (*Gen* 3:20). Aware that God has intervened, Eve exclaims: "I have begotten a man with the help of the Lord" (*Gen* 4:1). In procreation therefore, through the communication of life from parents to child, God's own image and likeness is transmitted, thanks to the creation of the immortal soul.[32] The beginning of the "book of the genealogy of Adam" expresses it in this way: "When God created man, he made him in the likeness of God. Male and female he created them, and he blessed them and called them man when they were created. When Adam had lived a hundred and thirty years, he became the father of a son in his own likeness, after his image, and named him Seth" (*Gen* 5:1-3). It is precisely in their role as co-workers with God *who transmits his image to the new creature* that we see the greatness of couples who are ready "to cooperate with the love of the Creator and the Saviour, who through them will enlarge and enrich his own family day by day".[33] This is why the Bishop Amphilochius extolled "holy matrimony, chosen and elevated above all other earthly gifts" as "the begetter of humanity, the creator of images of God".[34]

Thus, a man and woman joined in matrimony

become partners in a divine undertaking: through the act of procreation, God's gift is accepted and a new life opens to the future.

But over and above the specific mission of parents, *the task of accepting and serving life involves everyone; and this task must be fulfilled above all towards life when it is at its weakest.* It is Christ himself who reminds us of this when he asks to be loved and served in his brothers and sisters who are suffering in any way: the hungry, the thirsty, the foreigner, the naked, the sick, the imprisoned . . . Whatever is done to each of them is done to Christ himself (cf. *Mt* 25:31-46).

"For you formed my inmost being" (*Ps* 139:13): *the dignity of the unborn child*

44.   Human life finds itself most vulnerable when it enters the world and when it leaves the realm of time to embark upon eternity. The word of God frequently repeats the call to show care and respect, above all where life is undermined by sickness and old age. Although there are no direct and explicit calls to protect human life at its very beginning, specifically life not yet born, and life nearing its end, this can easily be explained by the fact that the mere possibility of harming,

attacking, or actually denying life in these circumstances is completely foreign to the religious and cultural way of thinking of the People of God.

In the Old Testament, sterility is dreaded as a curse, while numerous offspring are viewed as a blessing: "Sons are a heritage from the Lord, the fruit of the womb a reward" (*Ps* 127:3; cf. *Ps* 128:3-4). This belief is also based on Israel's awareness of being the people of the Covenant, called to increase in accordance with the promise made to Abraham: "Look towards heaven, and number the stars, if you are able to number them . . . so shall your descendants be" (*Gen* 15:5). But more than anything else, at work here is the certainty that the life which parents transmit has its origins in God. We see this attested in the many biblical passages which respectfully and lovingly speak of conception, of the forming of life in the mother's womb, of giving birth and of the intimate connection between the initial moment of life and the action of God the Creator.

"Before I formed you in the womb I knew you, and before you were born I consecrated you" (*Jer* 1:5): *the life of every individual, from its very beginning, is part of God's plan.* Job, from the depth of his pain, stops to contemplate the work of God who miraculously formed his body in his mother's womb. Here he finds reason for trust, and he expresses his belief that there is a divine plan for his life: "You have fashioned and made me; will you then turn and destroy me? Remember that you have made me of clay; and will you turn me to dust again? Did you not pour me out like milk and curdle me like cheese? You clothed me with skin and flesh, and knit me together with bones and sinews. You have granted me life and steadfast love; and your care has preserved my spirit" (*Job* 10:8-12). Expressions of awe and wonder at God's intervention in the life of a child in its mother's womb occur again and again in the Psalms.[35]

How can anyone think that even a single moment of this marvellous process of the unfolding of life could be separated from the wise and loving work of the Creator, and left prey to human caprice? Certainly the mother of the seven brothers did not think so; she professes her faith in God, both the source and guarantee of life from its very conception, and the foundation of the hope of new life beyond death: "I do not know how you came into being in my womb. It was not I who gave you life and breath, nor I who set in order the elements within each of you. Therefore the Creator of the world, who shaped the beginning of man and devised the origin of all things, will in his mercy give life and breath back to you again, since you now forget yourselves for the sake of his laws'' (*2 Mac* 7:22-23).

45.   The New Testament revelation confirms the *indisputable recognition of the value of life from its very beginning*. The exaltation of fruitfulness and the eager expectation of life resound in the words with which Elizabeth rejoices in her pregnancy: "The Lord has looked on me . . . to take away my reproach among men" (*Lk* 1:25). And even more so, the value of the person from the moment of conception is celebrated in the meeting between the Virgin Mary and Elizabeth, and between the two children whom they are carrying in the womb. It is precisely the children who reveal the advent of the Messianic age: in their meeting, the redemptive power of the presence of the Son of God among men first becomes operative. As Saint Ambrose writes: "The arrival of Mary and the blessings of the Lord's presence are also speedily declared . . . Elizabeth was the first to hear the voice; but John was the first to experience grace. She heard according to the order of nature; he leaped because of the mystery. She recognized the arrival of Mary; he the arrival of the Lord. The woman recognized the woman's arrival; the child, that of the child. The women speak of grace; the babies make it effective from

within to the advantage of their mothers who, by a double miracle, prophesy under the inspiration of their children. The infant leaped, the mother was filled with the Spirit. The mother was not filled before the son, but after the son was filled with the Holy Spirit, he filled his mother too".36

"I kept my faith even when I said, 'I am greatly afflicted' " (Ps 116:10): life in old age and at times of suffering

46.   With regard to the last moments of life too, it would be anachronistic to expect biblical revelation to make express reference to present-day issues concerning respect for elderly and sick persons, or to condemn explicitly attempts to hasten their end by force. The cultural and religious context of the Bible is in no way touched by such temptations; indeed, in that context the wisdom and experience of the elderly are recognized as a unique source of enrichment for the family and for society.

Old age is characterized by dignity and surrounded with reverence (cf. *2 Mac* 6:23). The just man does not seek to be delivered from old age and its burden; on the contrary his prayer is this: "You, O Lord, are my hope, my trust, O Lord, from my youth . . . so even to old age and grey hairs, O God, do not forsake me, till I proclaim your might to all the generations to come" (*Ps* 71:5, 18). The ideal of the Messianic age is presented as a time when "no more shall there be . . . an old man who does not fill out his days" (*Is* 65:20).

In old age, how should one face the inevitable decline of life? *How should one act in the face of death? The believer knows that his life is in the hands of God:* "You, O Lord, hold my lot" (cf. *Ps* 16:5), and he accepts from God the need to die: "This is the decree from the Lord for all flesh, and how can you reject the good pleasure of the Most High?" (*Sir* 41:3-4). Man is not the master of life, nor is he the master of death. In life and in death, he has to entrust himself completely to the "good pleasure of the Most High", to his loving plan.

In moments of *sickness* too, man is called to have the same trust in the Lord and to renew his fundamental faith in the One who "heals all your diseases" (cf. *Ps* 103:3). When every hope of good health seems to fade before a person's eyes —so as to make him cry out: "My days are like an evening shadow; I wither away like grass" (*Ps* 102:11)—even then the believer is sustained by an unshakable faith in God's life-giving power.

Illness does not drive such a person to despair and to seek death, but makes him cry out in hope: "I kept my faith, even when I said, 'I am greatly afflicted' " (*Ps* 116:10); "O Lord my God, I cried to you for help, and you have healed me. O Lord, you have brought up my soul from Sheol, restored me to life from among those gone down to the pit" (*Ps* 30:2-3).

47.   The mission of Jesus, with the many healings he performed, shows *God's great concern even for man's bodily life*. Jesus, as "the physician of the body and of the spirit",[37] was sent by the Father to proclaim the good news to the poor and to heal the brokenhearted (cf. *Lk* 4:18; *Is* 61:1). Later, when he sends his disciples into the world, he gives them a mission, a mission in which healing the sick goes hand in hand with the proclamation of the Gospel: "And preach as you go, saying, 'The kingdom of heaven is at hand'. Heal the sick, raise the dead, cleanse lepers, cast out demons" (*Mt* 10:7-8; cf. *Mk* 6:13; 16:18).

      Certainly *the life of the body in its earthly state is not an absolute good* for the believer, especially as he may be asked to give up his life for a greater good. As Jesus says: "Whoever would save his life will lose it; and whoever loses his life for my sake and the gospel's will save it'' (*Mk* 8:35). The New Testament gives many different examples of this. Jesus does not hesitate to sacrifice himself and he freely makes of his life an offering to the Father (cf. *Jn* 10:17) and to those who belong to him (cf. *Jn* 10:15). The death of John the Baptist, precursor of the Saviour, also testifies that earthly existence is not an absolute good; what is more important is remaining faithful to the word of the Lord even at the risk of one's life (cf. *Mk* 6:17-29). Stephen, losing his earthly life because of his faithful witness to the Lord's Resurrection, follows in the Master's footsteps and meets those who are stoning him with words of forgiveness (cf. *Acts* 7:59-60), thus becoming the first of a countless host of martyrs whom the Church has venerated since the very beginning.

No one, however, can arbitrarily choose whether to live or die; the absolute master of such a decision is the Creator alone, in whom ''we live and move and have our being'' (*Acts* 17:28).

"All who hold her fast will live" (Bar 4:1): from the law of Sinai to the gift of the Spirit

48. Life is indelibly marked by *a truth of its own*. By accepting God's gift, man is obliged to

maintain life in this truth which is essential to it. To detach oneself from this truth is to condemn oneself to meaninglessness and unhappiness, and possibly to become a threat to the existence of others, since the barriers guaranteeing respect for life and the defence of life, in every circumstance, have been broken down.

The truth of life is revealed by God's commandment. The word of the Lord shows concretely the course which life must follow if it is to respect its own truth and to preserve its own dignity. The protection of life is not only ensured by the specific commandment "You shall not kill" (*Ex* 20:13; *Dt* 5:17); *the entire Law of the Lord* serves to protect life, because it reveals that truth in which life finds its full meaning.

It is not surprising, therefore, that God's Covenant with his people is so closely linked to the perspective of life, also in its bodily dimension. In that Covenant, God's *commandment* is offered as *the path of life:* "I have set before you this day life and good, death and evil. If you obey the commandments of the Lord your God which I command you this day, by loving the Lord your God, by walking in his ways, and by keeping his commandments and his statutes and his ordinances, then you shall live and multiply, and the Lord your God will bless you in the land which you are entering to take possession of" (*Dt* 30:15-

16). What is at stake is not only the land of Canaan and the existence of the people of Israel, but also the world of today and of the future, and the existence of all humanity. In fact, it is altogether impossible for life to remain authentic and complete once it is detached from the good; and the good, in its turn, is essentially bound to the commandments of the Lord, that is, to the "law of life" (*Sir* 17:11). The good to be done is not added to life as a burden which weighs on it, since the very purpose of life is that good and only by doing it can life be built up.

It is thus *the Law as a whole* which fully protects human life. This explains why it is so hard to remain faithful to the commandment "You shall not kill" when the other "words of life" (cf. *Acts* 7:38) with which this commandment is bound up are not observed. Detached from this wider framework, the commandment is destined to become nothing more than an obligation imposed from without, and very soon we begin to look for its limits and try to find mitigating factors and exceptions. Only when people are open to the fullness of the truth about God, man and history will the words "You shall not kill" shine forth once more as a good for man in himself and in his relations with others. In such a perspective we can grasp the full truth of the passage of the Book of Deuteronomy which Jesus repeats in reply to the first temptation: "Man does not live by bread alone, but . . . by everything that proceeds out of the mouth of the Lord" (*Dt* 8:3; cf. *Mt* 4:4).

It is by listening to the word of the Lord that we are able to live in dignity and justice. It is by observing the Law of God that we are able to bring forth fruits of life and happiness: "All who hold her fast will live, and those who forsake her will die" (*Bar* 4:1).

49. The history of Israel shows how *difficult it is to remain faithful to the Law of life* which God has inscribed in human hearts and which he gave on Sinai to the people of the Covenant. When the people look for ways of living which ignore God's plan, it is the Prophets in particular who forcefully remind them that the Lord alone is the authentic source of life. Thus Jeremiah writes: "My people have committed two evils: they have forsaken me, the fountain of living waters, and hewed out cisterns for themselves, broken cisterns, that can hold no water" (2:13). The Prophets point an accusing finger at those who show contempt for life and violate people's rights: "They trample the head of the poor into the dust of the earth" (*Amos* 2:7); "they have filled this place with the blood of innocents" (*Jer* 19:4). Among them, the Prophet Ezekiel frequently con-

demns the city of Jerusalem, calling it "the bloody city" (22:2; 24:6, 9), the "city that sheds blood in her own midst" (22:3).

But while the Prophets condemn offences against life, they are concerned above all to awaken *hope for a new principle of life,* capable of bringing about a renewed relationship with God and with others, and of opening up new and extraordinary possibilities for understanding and carrying out all the demands inherent in the *Gospel of life*. This will only be possible thanks to the gift of God who purifies and renews: "I will sprinkle clean water upon you, and you shall be clean from all your uncleannesses, and from all your idols I will cleanse you. A new heart I will give you, and a new spirit I will put within you" (*Ezek* 36:25-26; cf. *Jer* 31:34). This "new heart" will make it possible to appreciate and achieve the deepest and most authentic meaning of life: namely, that of being *a gift which is fully realized in the giving of self*. This is the splendid message about the value of life which comes to us from the figure of the Servant of the Lord: "When he makes himself an offering for sin, he shall see his offspring, he shall prolong his life . . . he shall see the fruit of the travail of his soul and be satisfied" (*Is* 53:10, 11).

It is in the coming of Jesus of Nazareth that the Law is fulfilled and that a new heart is given through his Spirit. Jesus does not deny the Law but brings it to fulfilment (cf. *Mt* 5:17): the Law and the Prophets are summed up in the golden rule of mutual love (cf. *Mt* 7:12). In Jesus the Law becomes once and for all the "gospel", the good news of God's lordship over the world, which brings all life back to its roots and its original purpose. This is the *New Law*, "the law of the Spirit of life in Christ Jesus" (*Rom* 8:2), and its fundamental expression, following the example of the Lord who gave his life for his friends (cf. *Jn* 15:13), is *the gift of self in love for one's brothers and sisters:* "We know that we have passed out of death into life, because we love the brethren" (*1 Jn* 3:14). This is the law of freedom, joy and blessedness.

"They shall look on him whom they have pierced" (Jn 19:37): the Gospel of life is brought to fulfilment on the tree of the Cross

50.   At the end of this chapter, in which we have reflected on the Christian message about life, I would like to pause with each one of you to *contemplate the One who was pierced* and who draws all people to himself (cf. *Jn* 19:37; 12:32). Looking at "the spectacle" of the Cross (cf. *Lk* 23:48) we shall discover in this glorious tree the

fulfilment and the complete revelation of the whole *Gospel of life*.

In the early afternoon of Good Friday, "there was darkness over the whole land . . . while the sun's light failed; and the curtain of the temple was torn in two" (*Lk* 23:44, 45). This is the symbol of a great cosmic disturbance and a massive conflict between the forces of good and the forces of evil, between life and death. Today we too find ourselves in the midst of a dramatic conflict between the "culture of death" and the "culture of life". But the glory of the Cross is not overcome by this darkness; rather, it shines forth ever more radiantly and brightly, and is revealed as the centre, meaning and goal of all history and of every human life.

Jesus is nailed to the Cross and is lifted up from the earth. He experiences the moment of his greatest "powerlessness", and his life seems completely delivered to the derision of his adversaries and into the hands of his executioners: he is mocked, jeered at, insulted (cf. *Mk* 15:24-36). And yet, precisely amid all this, having seen him breathe his last, the Roman centurion exclaims: "Truly this man was the Son of God!" (*Mk* 15:39). It is thus, at the moment of his greatest weakness, that the the Son of God is revealed for who he is: *on the Cross his glory is made manifest*.

By his death, Jesus sheds light on the meaning of the life and death of every human being. Before he dies, Jesus prays to the Father, asking forgiveness for his persecutors (cf. *Lk* 23:34), and to the criminal who asks him to remember him in his kingdom he replies: "Truly, I say to you, today you will be with me in Paradise" (*Lk* 23:43). After his death "the tombs also were opened, and many bodies of the saints who had fallen asleep were raised" (*Mt* 27:52). The salvation wrought by Jesus is the bestowal of life and resurrection. Throughout his earthly life, Jesus had indeed bestowed salvation by healing and doing good to all (cf. *Acts* 10:38). But his miracles, healings and even his raising of the dead were signs of another salvation, a salvation which consists in the forgiveness of sins, that is, in setting man free from his greatest sickness and in raising him to the very life of God.

On the Cross, the miracle of the serpent lifted up by Moses in the desert (*Jn* 3:14-15; cf. *Num* 21:8-9) is renewed and brought to full and definitive perfection. Today too, by looking upon the one who was pierced, every person whose life is threatened encounters the sure hope of finding freedom and redemption.

51.   But there is yet another particular event which moves me deeply when I consider it.

"When Jesus had received the vinegar, he said, 'It is finished'; and he bowed his head and gave up his spirit" (*Jn* 19:30). Afterwards, the Roman soldier "pierced his side with a spear, and at once there came out blood and water" (*Jn* 19:34).

Everything has now reached its complete fulfilment. The "giving up" of the spirit describes Jesus' death, a death like that of every other human being, but it also seems to allude to the "gift of the Spirit", by which Jesus ransoms us from death and opens before us a new life.

It is the very life of God which is now shared with man. It is the life which through the Sacraments of the Church—symbolized by the blood and water flowing from Christ's side—is continually given to God's children, making them the people of the New Covenant. *From the Cross, the source of life, the "people of life" is born and increases.*

The contemplation of the Cross thus brings us to the very heart of all that has taken place. Jesus, who upon entering into the world said: "I have come, O God, to do your will" (cf. *Heb* 10:9), made himself obedient to the Father in everything and, "having loved his own who were in the world, he loved them to the end" (*Jn* 13:1), giving himself completely for them.

He who had come "not to be served but to serve, and to give his life as a ransom for many"

(*Mk* 10:45), attains on the Cross the heights of love: "Greater love has no man than this, that a man lay down his life for his friends" (*Jn* 15:13). And he died for us while we were yet sinners (cf. *Rom* 5:8).

In this way Jesus proclaims that *life finds its centre, its meaning and its fulfilment when it is given up.*

At this point our meditation becomes praise and thanksgiving, and at the same time urges us to imitate Christ and follow in his footsteps (cf. *1 Pt* 2:21).

We too are called to give our lives for our brothers and sisters, and thus to realize in the fullness of truth the meaning and destiny of our existence.

We shall be able to do this because you, O Lord, have given us the example and have bestowed on us the power of your Spirit. We shall be able to do this if every day, with you and like you, we are obedient to the Father and do his will.

Grant, therefore, that we may listen with open and generous hearts to every word which proceeds from the mouth of God. Thus we shall learn not only to obey the commandment not to kill human life, but also to revere life, to love it and to foster it.

CHAPTER III

YOU SHALL NOT KILL

GOD'S HOLY LAW

"If you would enter life, keep the commandments" (Mt 19:17): Gospel and commandment

52.　　"And behold, one came up to him, saying, 'Teacher, what good deed must I do, to have eternal life?' " (*Mt* 19:6). Jesus replied, "If you would enter life, keep the commandments" (*Mt* 19:17). The Teacher is speaking about eternal life, that is, a sharing in the life of God himself. This life is attained through the observance of the Lord's commandments, including the commandment "You shall not kill". This is the first precept from the Decalogue which Jesus quotes to the young man who asks him what commandments he should observe: "Jesus said, 'You shall not kill, You shall not commit adultery, You shall not steal . . .' " (*Mt* 19:18).

God's commandment is never detached from his love: it is always a gift meant for man's growth and joy. As such, it represents an essential and

107

indispensable aspect of the Gospel, actually becoming "gospel" itself: joyful good news. The *Gospel of life* is both a great gift of God and an exacting task for humanity. It gives rise to amazement and gratitude in the person graced with freedom, and it asks to be welcomed, preserved and esteemed, with a deep sense of responsibility. In giving life to man, God *demands* that he love, respect and promote life. *The gift* thus *becomes a commandment,* and *the commandment is itself a gift.*

Man, as the living image of God, is willed by his Creator to be ruler and lord. Saint Gregory of Nyssa writes that "God made man capable of carrying out his role as king of the earth . . . Man was created in the image of the One who governs the universe. Everything demonstrates that from the beginning man's nature was marked by royalty . . . Man is a king. Created to exercise dominion over the world, he was given a likeness to the king of the universe; he is the living image who participates by his dignity in the perfection of the divine archetype".[38] Called to be fruitful and multiply, to subdue the earth and to exercise dominion over other lesser creatures (cf. *Gen* 1:28), man is ruler and lord not only over things but especially over himself,[39] and in a certain sense, over the life which he has received and which he is able to transmit through procreation, carried out with love and respect for God's plan. Man's *lordship* however is not absolute, but *ministerial:* it is a real reflection of the unique and infinite lordship of God. Hence man must exercise it with *wisdom and love,* sharing in the boundless wisdom and love of God. And this comes about through obedience to God's holy Law: a free and joyful obedience (cf. *Ps* 119), born of and fostered by an awareness that the precepts of the Lord are a gift of grace entrusted to man always and solely for his good, for the preservation of his personal dignity and the pursuit of his happiness.

With regard to things, but even more with regard to life, man is not the absolute master and final judge, but rather—and this is where his incomparable greatness lies—he is the "minister of God's plan".[40]

Life is entrusted to man as a treasure which must not be squandered, as a talent which must be used well. Man must render an account of it to his Master (cf. *Mt* 25:14-30; *Lk* 19:12-27).

"From man in regard to his fellow man I will demand an accounting for human life" (Gen 9:5): human life is sacred and inviolable

53.   "Human life is sacred because from its beginning it involves 'the creative action of God', and it remains forever in a special relationship with the Creator, who is its sole end. God alone is the Lord of life from its beginning until its end: no one can, in any circumstance, claim for himself the right to destroy directly an innocent human being".41 With these words the Instruction *Donum Vitae* sets forth the central content of God's revelation on the sacredness and inviolability of human life.

Sacred Scripture in fact presents the precept "You shall not kill" as a divine commandment (*Ex* 20:13; *Dt* 5:17). As I have already emphasized, this commandment is found in the Decalogue, at the heart of the Covenant which the Lord makes with his chosen people; but it was already contained in the original covenant between God and humanity after the purifying punishment of the Flood, caused by the spread of sin and violence (cf. *Gen* 9:5-6).

God proclaims that he is absolute Lord of the life of man, who is formed in his image and likeness (cf. *Gen* 1:26-28). Human life is thus given a

110

sacred and inviolable character, which reflects the inviolability of the Creator himself. Precisely for this reason God will severely judge every violation of the commandment "You shall not kill", the commandment which is at the basis of all life together in society. He is the *"goel"*, the defender of the innocent (cf. *Gen* 4:9-15; *Is* 41:14; *Jer* 50:34; *Ps* 19:14). God thus shows that he does not delight in the death of the living (cf. *Wis* 1:13). Only Satan can delight therein: for through his envy death entered the world (cf. *Wis* 2:24). He who is "a murderer from the beginning", is also "a liar and the father of lies" (*Jn* 8:44). By deceiving man he leads him to projects of sin and death, making them appear as goals and fruits of life.

54.   As explicitly formulated, the precept "You shall not kill" is strongly negative: it indicates the extreme limit which can never be exceeded. Implicitly, however, it encourages a positive attitude of absolute respect for life; it leads to the promotion of life and to progress along the way of a love which gives, receives and serves. The people of the Covenant, although slowly and with some contradictions, progressively matured in this way of thinking, and thus prepared for the great proclamation of Jesus that the commandment to love one's neighbour is like

the commandment to love God; "on these two commandments depend all the law and the prophets" (cf. *Mt* 22:36-40). Saint Paul emphasizes that "the commandment . . . you shall not kill . . . and any other commandment, are summed up in this phrase: 'You shall love your neighbour as yourself' " (*Rom* 13:9; cf. *Gal* 5:14). Taken up and brought to fulfilment in the New Law, the commandment "You shall not kill" stands as an indispensable condition for being able "to enter life" (cf. *Mt* 19:16-19). In this same perspective, the words of the Apostle John have a categorical ring: "Anyone who hates his brother is a murderer, and you know that no murderer has eternal life abiding in him" (*1 Jn* 3:15).

From the beginning, the *living Tradition of the Church*—as shown by the *Didache,* the most ancient non-biblical Christian writing—categorically repeated the commandment "You shall not kill": "There are two ways, a way of life and a way of death; there is a great difference between them . . . In accordance with the precept of the teaching: you shall not kill . . . you shall not put a child to death by abortion nor kill it once it is born . . . The way of death is this: . . . they show no compassion for the poor, they do not suffer with the suffering, they do not acknowledge their Creator, they kill their children and by

112

abortion cause God's creatures to perish; they drive away the needy, oppress the suffering, they are advocates of the rich and unjust judges of the poor; they are filled with every sin. May you be able to stay ever apart, o children, from all these sins!''.[42]

As time passed, the Church's Tradition has always consistently taught the absolute and unchanging value of the commandment ''You shall not kill''. It is a known fact that in the first centuries, murder was put among the three most serious sins—along with apostasy and adultery—and required a particularly heavy and lengthy public penance before the repentant murderer could be granted forgiveness and readmission to the ecclesial community.

55.   This should not cause surprise: to kill a human being, in whom the image of God is present, is a particularly serious sin. *Only God is the master of life!* Yet from the beginning, faced with the many and often tragic cases which occur in the life of individuals and society, Christian reflection has sought a fuller and deeper understanding of what God's commandment prohibits and prescribes.[43] There are in fact situations in which values proposed by God's Law seem to involve a genuine paradox. This happens for ex-

ample in the case of *legitimate defence,* in which the right to protect one's own life and the duty not to harm someone else's life are difficult to reconcile in practice. Certainly, the intrinsic value of life and the duty to love oneself no less than others are the basis of *a true right to self-defence.* The demanding commandment of love of neighbour, set forth in the Old Testament and confirmed by Jesus, itself presupposes love of oneself as the basis of comparison: "You shall love your neighbour *as yourself*" (*Mk* 12:31). Consequently, no one can renounce the right to self-defence out of lack of love for life or for self. This can only be done in virtue of a heroic love which deepens and transfigures the love of self into a radical self-offering, according to the spirit of the Gospel Beatitudes (cf. *Mt* 5:38-40). The sublime example of this self-offering is the Lord Jesus himself.

Moreover, "legitimate defence can be not only a right but a grave duty for someone responsible for another's life, the common good of the family or of the State".[44] Unfortunately it happens that the need to render the aggressor incapable of causing harm sometimes involves taking his life. In this case, the fatal outcome is attributable to the aggressor whose action brought it about, even though he may not be morally responsible because of a lack of the use of reason.[45]

56.   This is the context in which to place the problem of the *death penalty*. On this matter there is a growing tendency, both in the Church and in civil society, to demand that it be applied in a very limited way or even that it be abolished completely. The problem must be viewed in the context of a system of penal justice ever more in line with human dignity and thus, in the end, with God's plan for man and society. The primary purpose of the punishment which society inflicts is "to redress the disorder caused by the offence".[46] Public authority must redress the violation of personal and social rights by imposing on the offender an adequate punishment for the crime, as a condition for the offender to regain the exercise of his or her freedom. In this way authority also fulfils the purpose of defending public order and ensuring people's safety, while at the same time offering the offender an incentive and help to change his or her behaviour and be rehabilitated.[47]

It is clear that, for these purposes to be achieved, *the nature and extent of the punishment* must be carefully evaluated and decided upon, and ought not go to the extreme of executing the offender except in cases of absolute necessity: in other words, when it would not be possible otherwise to defend society. Today however, as a result of steady improvements in the organization of the penal system, such cases are very rare, if not practically non-existent.

In any event, the principle set forth in the new *Catechism of the Catholic Church* remains valid: "If bloodless means are sufficient to defend human lives against an aggressor and to protect public order and the safety of persons, public authority must limit itself to such means, because they better correspond to the concrete conditions of the common good and are more in conformity to the dignity of the human person".[48]

57.   If such great care must be taken to respect every life, even that of criminals and unjust aggressors, the commandment "You shall not kill" has absolute value when it refers to the *innocent person*. And all the more so in the case of weak and defenceless human beings, who find their ultimate defence against the arrogance and caprice of others only in the absolute binding force of God's commandment.

In effect, the absolute inviolability of innocent human life is a moral truth clearly taught by

Sacred Scripture, constantly upheld in the Church's Tradition and consistently proposed by her Magisterium. This consistent teaching is the evident result of that "supernatural sense of the faith" which, inspired and sustained by the Holy Spirit, safeguards the People of God from error when "it shows universal agreement in matters of faith and morals".[49]

Faced with the progressive weakening in individual consciences and in society of the sense of the absolute and grave moral illicitness of the direct taking of all innocent human life, especially at its beginning and at its end, *the Church's Magisterium* has spoken out with increasing frequency in defence of the sacredness and inviolability of human life. The Papal Magisterium, particularly insistent in this regard, has always been seconded by that of the Bishops, with numerous and comprehensive doctrinal and pastoral documents issued either by Episcopal Conferences or by individual Bishops. The Second Vatican Council also addressed the matter forcefully, in a brief but incisive passage.[50]

Therefore, by the authority which Christ conferred upon Peter and his Successors, and in communion with the Bishops of the Catholic Church, *I confirm that the direct and voluntary killing of an innocent human being is always*

117

gravely immoral. This doctrine, based upon that unwritten law which man, in the light of reason, finds in his own heart (cf. *Rom* 2:14-15), is reaffirmed by Sacred Scripture, transmitted by the Tradition of the Church and taught by the ordinary and universal Magisterium.[51]

The deliberate decision to deprive an innocent human being of his life is always morally evil and can never be licit either as an end in itself or as a means to a good end. It is in fact a grave act of disobedience to the moral law, and indeed to God himself, the author and guarantor of that law; it contradicts the fundamental virtues of justice and charity. "Nothing and no one can in any way permit the killing of an innocent human being, whether a fetus or an embryo, an infant or an adult, an old person, or one suffering from an incurable disease, or a person who is dying. Furthermore, no one is permitted to ask for this act of killing, either for himself or herself or for another person entrusted to his or her care, nor can he or she consent to it, either explicitly or implicitly. Nor can any authority legitimately recommend or permit such an action".[52]

As far as the right to life is concerned, every innocent human being is absolutely equal to all others. This equality is the basis of all authentic social relationships which, to be truly such, can only be founded on truth and justice, recognizing and protecting every man and woman as a person and not as an object to be used. Before the moral norm which prohibits the direct taking of the life of an innocent human being "there are no privileges or exceptions for anyone. It makes no difference whether one is the master of the world or the 'poorest of the poor' on the face of the earth. Before the demands of morality we are all absolutely equal".[53]

"Your eyes beheld my unformed substance" (Ps 139:16): the unspeakable crime of abortion

58.   Among all the crimes which can be committed against life, procured abortion has characteristics making it particularly serious and deplorable. The Second Vatican Council defines abortion, together with infanticide, as an "unspeakable crime".[54]

But today, in many people's consciences, the perception of its gravity has become progressively obscured. The acceptance of abortion in the popular mind, in behaviour and even in law itself, is a telling sign of an extremely dangerous crisis of the moral sense, which is becoming more and more incapable of distinguishing between

119

good and evil, even when the fundamental right to life is at stake. Given such a grave situation, we need now more than ever to have the courage to look the truth in the eye and to *call things by their proper name,* without yielding to convenient compromises or to the temptation of self-deception. In this regard the reproach of the Prophet is extremely straightforward: "Woe to those who call evil good and good evil, who put darkness for light and light for darkness" (*Is* 5:20). Especially in the case of abortion there is a widespread use of ambiguous terminology, such as "interruption of pregnancy", which tends to hide abortion's true nature and to attenuate its seriousness in public opinion. Perhaps this linguistic phenomenon is itself a symptom of an uneasiness of conscience. But no word has the power to change the reality of things: procured abortion is *the deliberate and direct killing, by whatever means it is carried out, of a human being in the initial phase of his or her existence, extending from conception to birth.*

The moral gravity of procured abortion is apparent in all its truth if we recognize that we are dealing with murder and, in particular, when we consider the specific elements involved. The one eliminated is a human being at the very beginning of life. No one more absolutely *innocent* could be

120

imagined. In no way could this human being ever be considered an aggressor, much less an unjust aggressor! He or she is *weak,* defenceless, even to the point of lacking that minimal form of defence consisting in the poignant power of a newborn baby's cries and tears. The unborn child is *totally entrusted* to the protection and care of the woman carrying him or her in the womb. And yet sometimes it is precisely the mother herself who makes the decision and asks for the child to be eliminated, and who then goes about having it done.

It is true that the decision to have an abortion is often tragic and painful for the mother, insofar as the decision to rid herself of the fruit of conception is not made for purely selfish reasons or out of convenience, but out of a desire to protect certain important values such as her own health or a decent standard of living for the other members of the family. Sometimes it is feared that the child to be born would live in such conditions that it would be better if the birth did not take place. Nevertheless, these reasons and others like them, however serious and tragic, *can never justify the deliberate killing of an innocent human being.*

59.   As well as the mother, there are often other people too who decide upon the death of the child in the womb. In the first place, the father

of the child may be to blame, not only when he directly pressures the woman to have an abortion, but also when he indirectly encourages such a decision on her part by leaving her alone to face the problems of pregnancy:[55] in this way the family is thus mortally wounded and profaned in its nature as a community of love and in its vocation to be the ''sanctuary of life''. Nor can one overlook the pressures which sometimes come from the wider family circle and from friends. Sometimes the woman is subjected to such strong pressure that she feels psychologically forced to have an abortion: certainly in this case moral responsibility lies particularly with those who have directly or indirectly obliged her to have an abortion. Doctors and nurses are also responsible, when they place at the service of death skills which were acquired for promoting life.

But responsibility likewise falls on the legislators who have promoted and approved abortion laws, and, to the extent that they have a say in the matter, on the administrators of the health-care centres where abortions are performed. A general and no less serious responsibility lies with those who have encouraged the spread of an attitude of sexual permissiveness and a lack of esteem for motherhood, and with those who should have ensured—but did not—effective family and social policies in support of families, especially larger families and those with particular financial and educational needs. Finally, one cannot overlook the network of complicity which reaches out to include international institutions, foundations and associations which systematically campaign for the legalization and spread of abortion in the world. In this sense abortion goes beyond the responsibility of individuals and beyond the harm done to them, and takes on a distinctly social dimension. It is a most serious *wound* inflicted on society and its culture by the very people who ought to be society's promoters and defenders. As I wrote in my *Letter to Families,* "we are facing an immense threat to life: not only to the life of individuals but also to that of civilization itself".56 We are facing what can be called *a "structure of sin" which opposes human life not yet born.*

60.   Some people try to justify abortion by claiming that the result of conception, at least up to a certain number of days, cannot yet be considered a personal human life. But in fact, "from the time that the ovum is fertilized, a life is begun which is neither that of the father nor the mother; it is rather the life of a new human being with his own growth. It would never be made human if it

were not human already. This has always been clear, and . . . modern genetic science offers clear confirmation. It has demonstrated that from the first instant there is established the programme of what this living being will be: a person, this individual person with his characteristic aspects already well determined. Right from fertilization the adventure of a human life begins, and each of its capacities requires time—a rather lengthy time—to find its place and to be in a position to act".[57] Even if the presence of a spiritual soul cannot be ascertained by empirical data, the results themselves of scientific research on the human embryo provide "a valuable indication for discerning by the use of reason a personal presence at the moment of the first appearance of a human life: how could a human individual not be a human person?".[58]

Furthermore, what is at stake is so important that, from the standpoint of moral obligation, the mere probability that a human person is involved would suffice to justify an absolutely clear prohibition of any intervention aimed at killing a human embryo. Precisely for this reason, over and above all scientific debates and those philosophical affirmations to which the Magisterium has not expressly committed itself, the Church has always taught and continues to teach that the result of human procreation, from the first moment of its existence, must be guaranteed that unconditional respect which is morally due to the human being in his or her totality and unity as body and spirit: *"The human being is to be respected and treated as a person from the moment of conception;* and therefore from that same moment his rights as a person must be recognized, among which in the first place is the inviolable right of every innocent human being to life".[59]

61.   The texts of *Sacred Scripture* never address the question of deliberate abortion and so do not directly and specifically condemn it. But they show such great respect for the human being in the mother's womb that they require as a logical consequence that God's commandment "You shall not kill" be extended to the unborn child as well.

Human life is sacred and inviolable at every moment of existence, including the initial phase which precedes birth. All human beings, from their mothers' womb, belong to God who searches them and knows them, who forms them and knits them together with his own hands, who gazes on them when they are tiny shapeless embryos and already sees in them the adults of tomorrow whose days are numbered and whose vocation is even now written in the "book of life" (cf. *Ps* 139: 1, 13-16). There too, when they are still in their mothers' womb—as many passages of the Bible bear witness[60]—they are the personal objects of God's loving and fatherly providence.

Christian Tradition—as the *Declaration* issued by the Congregation for the Doctrine of the Faith points out so well[61]—is clear and unanimous, from the beginning up to our own day, in describing abortion as a particularly grave moral disorder. From its first contacts with the Greco-Roman world, where abortion and infanticide were widely practised, the first Christian community, by its teaching and practice, radically opposed the customs rampant in that society, as is clearly shown by the *Didache* mentioned earlier.[62] Among the Greek ecclesiastical writers, Athenagoras records that Christians consider as murderesses women who have recourse to abortifacient medicines, because children, even if they are still in their mother's womb, "are already under the protection of Divine Providence".[63] Among the Latin authors, Tertullian affirms: "It is anticipated murder to prevent someone from being born; it makes little difference whether one kills a soul already born or puts it to death at birth. He who will one day be a man is a man already".[64]

126

Throughout Christianity's two thousand year history, this same doctrine has been constantly taught by the Fathers of the Church and by her Pastors and Doctors. Even scientific and philosophical discussions about the precise moment of the infusion of the spiritual soul have never given rise to any hesitation about the moral condemnation of abortion.

62.   The more recent *Papal Magisterium* has vigorously reaffirmed this common doctrine. Pius XI in particular, in his Encyclical *Casti Connubii*, rejected the specious justifications of abortion.[65] Pius XII excluded all direct abortion, i.e., every act tending directly to destroy human life in the womb "whether such destruction is intended as an end or only as a means to an end".[66] John XXIII reaffirmed that human life is sacred because "from its very beginning it directly involves God's creative activity".[67] The Second Vatican Council, as mentioned earlier, sternly condemned abortion: "From the moment of its conception life must be guarded with the greatest care, while abortion and infanticide are unspeakable crimes".[68]

The *Church's canonical discipline,* from the earliest centuries, has inflicted penal sanctions on those guilty of abortion. This practice, with more or less severe penalties, has been confirmed in various periods of history. The 1917 *Code of Canon Law* punished abortion with excommunication.[69] The revised canonical legislation continues this tradition when it decrees that "a person who actually procures an abortion incurs automatic (*latae sententiae*) excommunication".[70] The excommunication affects all those who commit this crime with knowledge of the penalty attached, and thus includes those accomplices without whose help the crime would not have been committed.[71] By this reiterated sanction, the Church makes clear that abortion is a most serious and dangerous crime, thereby encouraging those who commit it to seek without delay the path of conversion. In the Church the purpose of the penalty of excommunication is to make an individual fully aware of the gravity of a certain sin and then to foster genuine conversion and repentance.

Given such unanimity in the doctrinal and disciplinary tradition of the Church, Paul VI was able to declare that this tradition is unchanged and unchangeable.[72] Therefore, by the authority which Christ conferred upon Peter and his Successors, in communion with the Bishops—who on various occasions have condemned abortion and who in the aforementioned consultation, albeit dispersed throughout the world, have shown unanimous agreement concerning this doctrine— *I declare that direct abortion, that is, abortion willed as an end or as a means, always constitutes a grave moral disorder*, since it is the deliberate killing of an innocent human being. This doctrine is based upon the natural law and upon the written Word of God, is transmitted by the Church's Tradition and taught by the ordinary and universal Magisterium.[73]

No circumstance, no purpose, no law whatsoever can ever make licit an act which is intrinsically illicit, since it is contrary to the Law of God which is written in every human heart, knowable by reason itself, and proclaimed by the Church.

63. This evaluation of the morality of abortion is to be applied also to the recent forms of *intervention on human embryos* which, although carried out for purposes legitimate in themselves, inevitably involve the killing of those embryos. This is the case with *experimentation on embryos*, which is becoming increasingly widespread in the field of biomedical research and is legally permitted in some countries. Although "one must uphold as licit procedures carried out on the human embryo which respect the life and integrity of the embryo and do not involve dispro-

portionate risks for it, but rather are directed to its healing, the improvement of its condition of health, or its individual survival",[74] it must nonetheless be stated that the use of human embryos or fetuses as an object of experimentation constitutes a crime against their dignity as human beings who have a right to the same respect owed to a child once born, just as to every person.[75]

This moral condemnation also regards procedures that exploit living human embryos and fetuses—sometimes specifically "produced" for this purpose by *in vitro* fertilization—either to be used as "biological material" or as *providers of organs or tissue for transplants* in the treatment of certain diseases. The killing of innocent human creatures, even if carried out to help others, constitutes an absolutely unacceptable act.

Special attention must be given to evaluating the morality of *prenatal diagnostic techniques* which enable the early detection of possible anomalies in the unborn child. In view of the complexity of these techniques, an accurate and systematic moral judgment is necessary. When they do not involve disproportionate risks for the child and the mother, and are meant to make possible early therapy or even to favour a serene and informed acceptance of the child not yet born, these techniques are morally licit. But since the possibilities of prenatal therapy are today still limited, it not infrequently happens that these techniques are used with a eugenic intention which accepts selective abortion in order to prevent the birth of children affected by various types of anomalies. Such an attitude is shameful and utterly reprehensible, since it presumes to measure the value of a human life only within the parameters of "normality" and physical well-being, thus opening the way to legitimizing infanticide and euthanasia as well.

And yet the courage and the serenity with which so many of our brothers and sisters suffering from serious disabilities lead their lives when they are shown acceptance and love bears eloquent witness to what gives authentic value to life, and makes it, even in difficult conditions, something precious for them and for others. The Church is close to those married couples who, with great anguish and suffering, willingly accept gravely handicapped children. She is also grateful to all those families which, through adoption, welcome children abandoned by their parents because of disabilities or illnesses.

"It is I who bring both death and life" (Dt 32:39): *the tragedy of euthanasia*

64.   At the other end of life's spectrum, men and women find themselves facing the mystery of death. Today, as a result of advances in medicine and in a cultural context frequently closed to the transcendent, the experience of dying is marked by new features. When the prevailing tendency is to value life only to the extent that it brings pleasure and well-being, suffering seems like an unbearable setback, something from which one must be freed at all costs. Death is considered "senseless" if it suddenly interrupts a life still open to a future of new and interesting experiences. But it becomes a "rightful liberation" once life is held to be no longer meaningful because it is filled with pain and inexorably doomed to even greater suffering.

Furthermore, when he denies or neglects his fundamental relationship to God, man thinks he is his own rule and measure, with the right to demand that society should guarantee him the ways and means of deciding what to do with his life in full and complete autonomy. It is especially people in the developed countries who act in this way: they feel encouraged to do so also by the constant progress of medicine and its ever more advanced techniques. By using highly sophisticated systems and equipment, science and medical practice today are able not only to attend to cases formerly considered untreatable and to reduce or eliminate pain, but also to sustain and prolong life even in situations of extreme frailty, to resuscitate artificially patients whose basic biological functions have undergone sudden collapse, and to use special procedures to make organs available for transplanting.

In this context the temptation grows to have recourse to *euthanasia,* that is, *to take control of death and bring it about before its time,* "gently" ending one's own life or the life of others. In reality, what might seem logical and humane, when looked at more closely is seen to be *senseless and inhumane.* Here we are faced with one of the more alarming symptoms of the "culture of death", which is advancing above all in prosperous societies, marked by an attitude of excessive preoccupation with efficiency and which sees the growing number of elderly and disabled people as intolerable and too burdensome. These people are very often isolated by their families and by society, which are organized almost exclusively on the basis of criteria of productive efficiency, according to which a hopelessly impaired life no longer has any value.

65.   For a correct moral judgment on euthanasia, in the first place a clear definition is required. *Euthanasia in the strict sense* is understood to be an action or omission which of itself and by intention causes death, with the purpose of eliminating all suffering. "Euthanasia's terms of reference, therefore, are to be found in the intention of the will and in the methods used".[76]

Euthanasia must be distinguished from the decision to forego so-called "aggressive medical treatment", in other words, medical procedures which no longer correspond to the real situation of the patient, either because they are by now disproportionate to any expected results or because they impose an excessive burden on the patient and his family. In such situations, when death is clearly imminent and inevitable, one can in conscience "refuse forms of treatment that would only secure a precarious and burdensome prolongation of life, so long as the normal care due to the sick person in similar cases is not interrupted".[77] Certainly there is a moral obligation to care for oneself and to allow oneself to be cared for, but this duty must take account of concrete circumstances. It needs to be determined whether the means of treatment available are objectively proportionate to the prospects for improvement. To forego extraordinary or disproportionate means is not the equivalent of suicide or euthanasia; it rather expresses acceptance of the human condition in the face of death.[78]

In modern medicine, increased attention is being given to what are called "methods of palliative care", which seek to make suffering more bearable in the final stages of illness and to ensure that the patient is supported and accompanied in his or her ordeal. Among the questions which arise in this context is that of the licitness of using various types of painkillers and sedatives for relieving the patient's pain when this involves the risk of shortening life. While praise may be due to the person who voluntarily accepts suffering by forgoing treatment with painkillers in order to remain fully lucid and, if a believer, to share consciously in the Lord's Passion, such "heroic" behaviour cannot be considered the duty of everyone. Pius XII affirmed that it is licit to relieve pain by narcotics, even when the result is decreased consciousness and a shortening of life, "if no other means exist, and if, in the given circumstances, this does not prevent the carrying out of other religious and moral duties".[79] In such a case, death is not willed or sought, even though for reasonable motives one runs the risk of it: there is simply a desire to ease pain effectively by using the analgesics which medicine provides. All the same, "it is not right to deprive the dying person of consciousness without a serious reason": [80] as they approach death people ought to be able to satisfy their moral and family duties, and above all they ought to be able to prepare in a fully conscious way for their definitive meeting with God.

Taking into account these distinctions, in harmony with the Magisterium of my Predecessors [81] and in communion with the Bishops of the Catholic Church, *I confirm that euthanasia is a grave violation of the law of God,* since it is the deliberate and morally unacceptable killing of a human person. This doctrine is based upon the natural law and upon the written word of God, is transmitted by the Church's Tradition and taught by the ordinary and universal Magisterium.[82]

Depending on the circumstances, this practice involves the malice proper to suicide or murder.

66.   Suicide is always as morally objectionable as murder. The Church's tradition has always rejected it as a gravely evil choice.[83] Even though a certain psychological, cultural and social conditioning may induce a person to carry out an action which so radically contradicts the innate inclination to life, thus lessening or removing subjective

responsibility, *suicide,* when viewed objectively, is a gravely immoral act. In fact, it involves the rejection of love of self and the renunciation of the obligation of justice and charity towards one's neighbour, towards the communities to which one belongs, and towards society as a whole.[84] In its deepest reality, suicide represents a rejection of God's absolute sovereignty over life and death, as proclaimed in the prayer of the ancient sage of Israel: "You have power over life and death; you lead men down to the gates of Hades and back again" (*Wis* 16:13; cf. *Tob* 13:2).

To concur with the intention of another person to commit suicide and to help in carrying it out through so-called "assisted suicide" means to cooperate in, and at times to be the actual perpetrator of, an injustice which can never be excused, even if it is requested. In a remarkably relevant passage Saint Augustine writes that "it is never licit to kill another: even if he should wish it, indeed if he request it because, hanging between life and death, he begs for help in freeing the soul struggling against the bonds of the body and longing to be released; nor is it licit even when a sick person is no longer able to live".[85] Even when not motivated by a selfish refusal to be burdened with the life of someone who is suffering, euthanasia must be called a *false mercy,* and indeed a disturbing "perversion" of mercy. True "compassion" leads to sharing another's pain; it does not kill the person whose suffering we cannot bear. Moreover, the act of euthanasia appears all the more perverse if it is carried out by those, like relatives, who are supposed to treat a family member with patience and love, or by those, such as doctors, who by virtue of their specific profession are supposed to care for the sick person even in the most painful terminal stages.

The choice of euthanasia becomes more serious when it takes the form of a *murder* committed by others on a person who has in no way requested it and who has never consented to it. The height of arbitrariness and injustice is reached when certain people, such as physicians or legislators, arrogate to themselves the power to decide who ought to live and who ought to die. Once again we find ourselves before the temptation of Eden: to become like God who "knows good and evil" (cf. *Gen* 3:5). God alone has the power over life and death: "It is I who bring both death and life" (*Dt* 32:39; cf. *2 Kg* 5:7; *1 Sam* 2:6). But he only exercises this power in accordance with a plan of wisdom and love. When man usurps this power, being enslaved by a foolish and selfish way of thinking, he inevitably uses it for injustice and death. Thus the life of the person who is weak is put into the hands of the one who is strong; in society the sense of justice is lost, and mutual trust, the basis of every authentic interpersonal relationship, is undermined at its root.

67.   Quite different from this is the *way of love and true mercy,* which our common humanity calls for, and upon which faith in Christ the Redeemer, who died and rose again, sheds ever new light. The request which arises from the human heart in the supreme confrontation with suffering and death, especially when faced with the temptation to give up in utter desperation, is above all a request for companionship, sympathy and support in the time of trial. It is a plea for help to keep on hoping when all human hopes fail. As the Second Vatican Council reminds us: "It is in the face of death that the riddle of human existence becomes most acute" and yet "man rightly follows the intuition of his heart when he abhors and repudiates the absolute ruin and total disappearance of his own person. Man rebels against death because he bears in himself an eternal seed which cannot be reduced to mere matter".[86]

This natural aversion to death and this incipient hope of immortality are illumined and brought to fulfilment by Christian faith, which both promises and offers a share in the victory of the Risen Christ: it is the victory of the One who, by his redemptive death, has set man free from death, "the wages of sin" (*Rom* 6:23), and has given him the Spirit, the pledge of resurrection and of life (cf. *Rom* 8:11). The certainty of future immortality and *hope in the promised resurrection* cast new light on the mystery of suffering and death, and fill the believer with an extraordinary capacity to trust fully in the plan of God.

The Apostle Paul expressed this newness in terms of belonging completely to the Lord who embraces every human condition: "None of us lives to himself, and none of us dies to himself. If we live, we live to the Lord, and if we die, we die to the Lord; so then, whether we live or whether we die, we are the Lord's" (*Rom* 14:7-8). *Dying to the Lord* means experiencing one's death as the supreme act of obedience to the Father (cf. *Phil* 2:8), being ready to meet death at the "hour" willed and chosen by him (cf. *Jn* 13:1), which can only mean when one's earthly pilgrimage is completed. *Living to the Lord* also means recognizing that suffering, while still an evil and a trial in itself, can always become a source of good. It becomes such if it is experienced for love and with love through sharing, by God's gracious gift and one's own personal and free choice, in the suffering of Christ Crucified. In this way, the person who lives his suffering in the Lord grows more fully conformed to him (cf. *Phil* 3:10; *1 Pet* 2:21) and more closely associated with his redemptive work on behalf of the Church and humanity.[87] This was the experience of Saint Paul, which every person who suffers is called to relive: "I rejoice in my sufferings for your sake, and in my flesh I complete what is lacking in Christ's afflictions for the sake of his Body, that is, the Church" (*Col* 1:24).

"We must obey God rather than men" (*Acts* 5:29): *civil law and the moral law*

68.   One of the specific characteristics of present-day attacks on human life—as has already been said several times—consists in the trend to demand a *legal justification* for them, as if they were rights which the State, at least under certain conditions, must acknowledge as belonging to citizens. Consequently, there is a tendency to claim that it should be possible to exercise these rights with the safe and free assistance of doctors and medical personnel.

It is often claimed that the life of an unborn child or a seriously disabled person is only a rela-

141

tive good: according to a proportionalist approach, or one of sheer calculation, this good should be compared with and balanced against other goods. It is even maintained that only someone present and personally involved in a concrete situation can correctly judge the goods at stake: consequently, only that person would be able to decide on the morality of his choice. The State therefore, in the interest of civil coexistence and social harmony, should respect this choice, even to the point of permitting abortion and euthanasia.

At other times, it is claimed that civil law cannot demand that all citizens should live according to moral standards higher than what all citizens themselves acknowledge and share. Hence the law should always express the opinion and will of the majority of citizens and recognize that they have, at least in certain extreme cases, the right even to abortion and euthanasia. Moreover the prohibition and the punishment of abortion and euthanasia in these cases would inevitably lead—so it is said—to an increase of illegal practices: and these would not be subject to necessary control by society and would be carried out in a medically unsafe way. The question is also raised whether supporting a law which in practice cannot be enforced would not ultimately undermine the authority of all laws.

Finally, the more radical views go so far as to maintain that in a modern and pluralistic society people should be allowed complete freedom to dispose of their own lives as well as of the lives of the unborn: it is asserted that it is not the task of the law to choose between different moral opinions, and still less can the law claim to impose one particular opinion to the detriment of others.

69.   In any case, in the democratic culture of our time it is commonly held that the legal system of any society should limit itself to taking account of and accepting the convictions of the majority. It should therefore be based solely upon what the majority itself considers moral and actually practises. Furthermore, if it is believed that an objective truth shared by all is *de facto* unattainable, then respect for the freedom of the citizens—who in a democratic system are considered the true rulers—would require that on the legislative level the autonomy of individual consciences be acknowledged. Consequently, when establishing those norms which are absolutely necessary for social coexistence, the only determining factor should be the will of the majority, whatever this may be. Hence every politician, in his or her activity, should clearly separate the realm of private conscience from that of public conduct.

As a result we have what appear to be two diametrically opposed tendencies. On the one hand, individuals claim for themselves in the moral sphere the most complete freedom of choice and demand that the State should not adopt or impose any ethical position but limit itself to guaranteeing maximum space for the freedom of each individual, with the sole limitation of not infringing on the freedom and rights of any other citizen. On the other hand, it is held that, in the exercise of public and professional duties, respect for other people's freedom of choice requires that each one should set aside his or her own convictions in order to satisfy every demand of the citizens which is recognized and guaranteed by law; in carrying out one's duties the only moral criterion should be what is laid down by the law itself. Individual responsibility is thus turned over to the civil law, with a renouncing of personal conscience, at least in the public sphere.

70.   At the basis of all these tendencies lies the *ethical relativism* which characterizes much of present-day culture. There are those who consider such relativism an essential condition of democracy, inasmuch as it alone is held to guarantee tolerance, mutual respect between people and acceptance of the decisions of the major-

ity, whereas moral norms considered to be objective and binding are held to lead to authoritarianism and intolerance.

But it is precisely the issue of respect for life which shows what misunderstandings and contradictions, accompanied by terrible practical consequences, are concealed in this position.

It is true that history has known cases where crimes have been committed in the name of "truth". But equally grave crimes and radical denials of freedom have also been committed and are still being committed in the name of "ethical relativism". When a parliamentary or social majority decrees that it is legal, at least under certain conditions, to kill unborn human life, is it not really making a "tyrannical" decision with regard to the weakest and most defenceless of human beings? Everyone's conscience rightly rejects those crimes against humanity of which our century has had such sad experience. But would these crimes cease to be crimes if, instead of being committed by unscrupulous tyrants, they were legitimated by popular consensus?

Democracy cannot be idolized to the point of making it a substitute for morality or a panacea for immorality. Fundamentally, democracy is a "system" and as such is a means and not an end. Its "moral" value is not automatic, but depends on conformity to the moral law to which it, like every other form of human behaviour, must be subject: in other words, its morality depends on the morality of the ends which it pursues and of the means which it employs. If today we see an almost universal consensus with regard to the value of democracy, this is to be considered a positive "sign of the times", as the Church's Magisterium has frequently noted.[88] But the value of democracy stands or falls with the values which it embodies and promotes. Of course, values such as the dignity of every human person, respect for inviolable and inalienable human rights, and the adoption of the "common good" as the end and criterion regulating political life are certainly fundamental and not to be ignored.

The basis of these values cannot be provisional and changeable "majority" opinions, but only the acknowledgment of an objective moral law which, as the "natural law" written in the human heart, is the obligatory point of reference for civil law itself. If, as a result of a tragic obscuring of the collective conscience, an attitude of scepticism were to succeed in bringing into question even the fundamental principles of the moral law, the democratic system itself would be shaken in its foundations, and would be reduced to a mere mechanism for regulating different and opposing interests on a purely empirical basis.[89]

Some might think that even this function, in the absence of anything better, should be valued for the sake of peace in society. While one acknowledges some element of truth in this point of view, it is easy to see that without an objective moral grounding not even democracy is capable of ensuring a stable peace, especially since peace which is not built upon the values of the dignity of every individual and of solidarity between all people frequently proves to be illusory. Even in participatory systems of government, the regulation of interests often occurs to the advantage of the most powerful, since they are the ones most capable of manoeuvering not only the levers of power but also of shaping the formation of consensus. In such a situation, democracy easily be comes an empty word.

71.   It is therefore urgently necessary, for the future of society and the development of a sound democracy, to rediscover those essential and innate human and moral values which flow from the very truth of the human being and express and safeguard the dignity of the person: values which no individual, no majority and no State can ever

create, modify or destroy, but must only acknowledge, respect and promote.

Consequently there is a need to recover the *basic elements of a vision of the relationship between civil law and moral law,* which are put forward by the Church, but which are also part of the patrimony of the great juridical traditions of humanity.

Certainly *the purpose of civil law* is different and more limited in scope than that of the moral law. But "in no sphere of life can the civil law take the place of conscience or dictate norms concerning things which are outside its competence",[90] which is that of ensuring the common good of people through the recognition and defence of their fundamental rights, and the promotion of peace and of public morality.[91] The real purpose of civil law is to guarantee an ordered social coexistence in true justice, so that all may "lead a quiet and peaceable life, godly and respectful in every way" (*1 Tim* 2:2). Precisely for this reason, civil law must ensure that all members of society enjoy respect for certain fundamental rights which innately belong to the person, rights which every positive law must recognize and guarantee. First and fundamental among these is the inviolable right to life of every innocent human being. While public authority can sometimes choose not to put a stop to something which—were it prohibited—would cause more serious harm,[92] it can never presume to legitimize as a right of individuals—even if they are the majority of the members of society—an offence against other persons caused by the disregard of so fundamental a right as the right to life. The legal toleration of abortion or of euthanasia can in no way claim to be based on respect for the conscience of others, precisely because society has the right and the duty to protect itself against the abuses which can occur in the name of conscience and under the pretext of freedom.[93]

In the Encyclical *Pacem in Terris*, John XXIII pointed out that "it is generally accepted today that the common good is best safeguarded when personal rights and duties are guaranteed. The chief concern of civil authorities must therefore be to ensure that these rights are recognized, respected, co-ordinated, defended and promoted, and that each individual is enabled to perform his duties more easily. For 'to safeguard the inviolable rights of the human person, and to facilitate the performance of his duties, is the principal duty of every public authority'. Thus any government which refused to recognize human rights or acted in violation of them, would not only fail in its duty; its decrees would be wholly lacking in binding force".[94]

72.   The doctrine on the necessary *conformity of civil law with the moral law* is in continuity with the whole tradition of the Church. This is clear once more from John XXIII's Encyclical: "Authority is a postulate of the moral order and derives from God. Consequently, laws and decrees enacted in contravention of the moral order, and hence of the divine will, can have no binding force in conscience . . . ; indeed, the passing of such laws undermines the very nature of authority and results in shameful abuse".[95] This is the clear teaching of Saint Thomas Aquinas, who writes that "human law is law inasmuch as it is in conformity with right reason and thus derives from the eternal law. But when a law is contrary to reason, it is called an unjust law; but in this case it ceases to be a law and becomes instead an act of violence".[96] And again: "Every law made by man can be called a law insofar as it derives from the natural law. But if it is somehow opposed to the natural law, then it is not really a law but rather a corruption of the law".[97]

Now the first and most immediate application of this teaching concerns a human law which disregards the fundamental right and source of all other rights which is the right to life, a right belonging to every individual. Consequently, laws which legitimize the direct killing of innocent human beings through abortion or euthanasia are in complete opposition to the inviolable right to life proper to every individual; they thus deny the equality of everyone before the law. It might be objected that such is not the case in euthanasia, when it is requested with full awareness by the person involved. But any State which made such a request legitimate and authorized it to be carried out would be legalizing a case of suicide-murder, contrary to the fundamental principles of absolute respect for life and of the protection of every innocent life. In this way the State contributes to lessening respect for life and opens the door to ways of acting which are destructive of trust in relations between people. Laws which authorize and promote abortion and euthanasia are therefore radically opposed not only to the good of the individual but also to the common good; as such they are completely lacking in authentic juridical validity. Disregard for the right to life, precisely because it leads to the killing of the person whom society exists to serve, is what most directly conflicts with the possibility of achieving the common good. Consequently, a civil law authorizing abortion or euthanasia ceases by that very fact to be a true, morally binding civil law.

73.   Abortion and euthanasia are thus crimes which no human law can claim to legitimize. There is no obligation in conscience to obey such laws; instead there is a *grave and clear obligation to oppose them by conscientious objection*. From the very beginnings of the Church, the apostolic preaching reminded Christians of their duty to obey legitimately constituted public authorities (cf. *Rom* 13:1-7; *1 Pet* 2:13-14), but at the same time it firmly warned that "we must obey God rather than men". (*Acts* 5:29). In the Old Testament, precisely in regard to threats against life, we find a significant example of resistance to the unjust command of those in authority. After Pharaoh ordered the killing of all newborn males, the Hebrew midwives refused. "They did not do as the king of Egypt commanded them, but let the male children live" (*Ex* 1:17). But the ultimate reason for their action should be noted: *"the midwives feared God"* (*ibid.*). It is precisely from obedience to God—to whom alone is due that fear which is acknowledgment of his absolute sovereignty—that the strength and the courage to resist unjust human laws are born. It is the strength and the courage of those prepared even

to be imprisoned or put to the sword, in the certainty that this is what makes for "the endurance and faith of the saints" (*Rev* 13:10).

In the case of an intrinsically unjust law, such as a law permitting abortion or euthanasia, it is therefore never licit to obey it, or to "take part in a propaganda campaign in favour of such a law, or vote for it.".[98]

A particular problem of conscience can arise in cases where a legislative vote would be decisive for the passage of a more restrictive law, aimed at limiting the number of authorized abortions, in place of a more permissive law already passed or ready to be voted on. Such cases are not infrequent. It is a fact that while in some parts of the world there continue to be campaigns to introduce laws favouring abortion, often supported by powerful international organizations, in other nations—particularly those which have already experienced the bitter fruits of such permissive legislation—there are growing signs of a rethinking in this matter. In a case like the one just mentioned, when it is not possible to overturn or completely abrogate a pro-abortion law, an elected official, whose absolute personal opposition to procured abortion was well known, could licitly support proposals aimed at *limiting the harm* done by such a law and at lessening its negative consequences at the level of general opinion and public morality. This does not in fact represent an illicit cooperation with an unjust law, but rather a legitimate and proper attempt to limit its evil aspects.

74.   The passing of unjust laws often raises difficult problems of conscience for morally upright people with regard to the issue of cooperation, since they have a right to demand not to be forced to take part in morally evil actions. Sometimes the choices which have to be made are difficult; they may require the sacrifice of prestigious professional positions or the relinquishing of reasonable hopes of career advancement. In other cases, it can happen that carrying out certain actions, which are provided for by legislation that overall is unjust, but which in themselves are indifferent, or even positive, can serve to protect human lives under threat. There may be reason to fear, however, that willingness to carry out such actions will not only cause scandal and weaken the necessary opposition to attacks on life, but will gradually lead to further capitulation to a mentality of permissiveness.

In order to shed light on this difficult question, it is necessary to recall the general principles concerning *cooperation in evil actions*. Christians, like all people of good will, are called upon under grave obligation of conscience not to cooperate formally in practices which, even if permitted by civil legislation, are contrary to God's law. Indeed, from the moral standpoint, it is never licit to cooperate formally in evil. Such cooperation occurs when an action, either by its very nature or by the form it takes in a concrete situation, can be defined as a direct participation in an act against innocent human life or a sharing in the immoral intention of the person committing it. This cooperation can never be justified either by invoking respect for the freedom of others or by appealing to the fact that civil law permits it or requires it. Each individual in fact has moral responsibility for the acts which he personally performs; no one can be exempted from this responsibility, and on the basis of it everyone will be judged by God himself (cf. *Rom* 2:6; 14:12).

To refuse to take part in committing an injustice is not only a moral duty; it is also a basic human right. Were this not so, the human person would be forced to perform an action intrinsically incompatible with human dignity, and in this way human freedom itself, the authentic meaning and purpose of which are found in its orientation to the true and the good, would be radically compromised. What is at stake therefore is an essential right which, precisely as such, should be acknowledged and protected by civil law. In this sense, the opportunity to refuse to take part in the phases of consultation, preparation and execution of these acts against life should be guaranteed to physicians, health-care personnel, and directors of hospitals, clinics and convalescent facilities. Those who have recourse to conscientious objection must be protected not only from legal penalties but also from any negative effects on the legal, disciplinary, financial and professional plane.

"You shall love your neighbour as yourself" (*Lk* 10:27): *"promote"* life

75.   God's commandments teach us the way of life. *The negative moral precepts,* which declare that the choice of certain actions is morally unacceptable, have an absolute value for human freedom: they are valid always and everywhere, without exception. They make it clear that the choice of certain ways of acting is radically incompatible with the love of God and with the dignity of the person created in his image. Such choices cannot be redeemed by the goodness of any intention or of any consequence; they are

156

irrevocably opposed to the bond between persons; they contradict the fundamental decision to direct one's life to God.[99]

In this sense, the negative moral precepts have an extremely important positive function. The "no" which they unconditionally require makes clear the absolute limit beneath which free individuals cannot lower themselves. At the same time they indicate the minimum which they must respect and from which they must start out in order to say "yes" over and over again, a "yes" which will gradually embrace the *entire horizon of the good* (cf. *Mt* 5:48). The commandments, in particular the negative moral precepts, are the beginning and the first necessary stage of the journey towards freedom. As Saint Augustine writes, "the beginning of freedom is to be free from crimes . . . like murder, adultery, fornication, theft, fraud, sacrilege and so forth. Only when one stops committing these crimes (and no Christian should commit them), one begins to lift up one's head towards freedom. But this is only the beginning of freedom, not perfect freedom".[100]

76.   The commandment "You shall not kill" thus establishes the point of departure for the start of true freedom. It leads us to promote life actively, and to develop particular ways of think-

ing and acting which serve life. In this way we exercise our responsibility towards the persons entrusted to us and we show, in deeds and in truth, our gratitude to God for the great gift of life (cf. *Ps* 139:13-14).

The Creator has entrusted man's life to his responsible concern, not to make arbitrary use of it, but to preserve it with wisdom and to care for it with loving fidelity. The God of the Covenant has entrusted the life of every individual to his or her fellow human beings, brothers and sisters, according to the law of reciprocity in giving and receiving, of self-giving and of the acceptance of others. In the fullness of time, by taking flesh and giving his life for us, the Son of God showed what heights and depths this law of reciprocity can reach. With the gift of his Spirit, Christ gives new content and meaning to the law of reciprocity, to our being entrusted to one another. The Spirit who builds up communion in love creates between us a new fraternity and solidarity, a true reflection of the mystery of mutual self-giving and receiving proper to the Most Holy Trinity. The Spirit becomes the new law which gives strength to believers and awakens in them a responsibility for sharing the gift of self and for accepting others, as a sharing in the boundless love of Jesus Christ himself.

77.   This new law also gives spirit and shape to the commandment "You shall not kill". For the Christian it involves an absolute imperative to respect, love and promote the life of every brother and sister, in accordance with the requirements of God's bountiful love in Jesus Christ. "He laid down his life for us; and we ought to lay down our lives for the brethren" (*1 Jn* 3:16).

The commandment "You shall not kill", even in its more positive aspects of respecting, loving and promoting human life, is binding on every individual human being. It resounds in the moral conscience of everyone as an irrepressible echo of the original covenant of God the Creator with mankind. It can be recognized by everyone through the light of reason and it can be observed thanks to the mysterious working of the Spirit who, blowing where he wills (cf. *Jn* 3:8), comes to and involves every person living in this world.

It is therefore a service of love which we are all committed to ensure to our neighbour, that his or her life may be always defended and promoted, especially when it is weak or threatened. It is not only a personal but a social concern which we must all foster: a concern to make unconditional respect for human life the foundation of a renewed society.

We are asked to love and honour the life of

every man and woman and to work with per-
severance and courage so that our time, marked
by all too many signs of death, may at last witness
the establishment of a new culture of life, the fruit
of the culture of truth and of love.

CHAPTER IV

YOU DID IT TO ME

FOR A NEW CULTURE OF HUMAN LIFE

"You are God's own people, that you may declare the wonderful deeds of him who called you out of darkness into his marvellous light" (1 Pet 2:9): *a people of life and for life*

78.   The Church has received the Gospel as a proclamation and a source of joy and salvation. She has received it as a gift from Jesus, sent by the Father "to preach good news to the poor" (*Lk* 4:18). She has received it through the Apostles, sent by Christ to the whole world (cf. *Mk* 16:15; *Mt* 28:19-20). Born from this evangelizing activity, the Church hears every day the echo of Saint Paul's words of warning: "Woe to me if I do not preach the Gospel!" (*1 Cor* 9:16). As Paul VI wrote, *"evangelization is the grace and vocation proper to the Church, her deepest identity. She exists in order to evangelize"*.[101]

Evangelization is an all-embracing, progressive activity through which the Church participates in the prophetic, priestly and royal mission of the Lord Jesus. It is therefore inextricably linked to *preaching, celebration and the service of charity*. Evangelization is a *profoundly ecclesial act*, which calls all the various workers of the Gospel to action, according to their individual charisms and ministry.

This is also the case with regard to the proclamation of the Gospel of life, an integral part of that Gospel which is Jesus Christ himself. We are at the service of this Gospel, sustained by the awareness that we have received it as a gift and are sent to preach it to all humanity, "to the ends of the earth" (*Acts* 1:8). With humility and gratitude we know that we are the *people of life and for life*, and this is how we present ourselves to everyone.

79.   We are the *people of life* because God, in his unconditional love, has given us the *Gospel of life* and by this same Gospel we have been transformed and saved. We have been ransomed by the "Author of life" (*Acts* 3:15) at the price of his precious blood (cf. *1 Cor* 6:20; 7:23; *1 Pet* 1:19). Through the waters of Baptism we have been made a part of him (cf. *Rom* 6:4-5; *Col* 2:12), as branches which draw nourishment and fruitfulness from the one tree (cf. *Jn* 15:5). Interiorly

renewed by the grace of the Spirit, "who is the Lord and giver of life", we have become a *people for life* and we are called to act accordingly.

We have been sent. For us, being at the service of life is not a boast but rather a duty, born of our awareness of being "God's own people, that we may declare the wonderful deeds of him who called us out of darkness into his marvellous light" (cf. *1 Pet* 2:9). On our journey *we are guided and sustained by the law of love:* a love which has as its source and model the Son of God made man, who "by dying gave life to the world".[102]

We have been sent as a people. Everyone has an obligation to be at the service of life. This is a properly "ecclesial" responsibility, which requires concerted and generous action by all the members and by all sectors of the Christian community. This community commitment does not however eliminate or lessen the responsibility of each *individual,* called by the Lord to "become the neighbour" of everyone: "Go and do likewise" (*Lk* 10:37).

Together we all sense our duty to *preach the Gospel of life,* to *celebrate it* in the Liturgy and in our whole existence, and to *serve it* with the various programmes and structures which support and promote life.

"That which we have seen and heard we proclaim also to you" (1 Jn 1:3): proclaiming the Gospel of life

80.   "That which was from the beginning, which we have heard, which we have seen with our eyes, which we have looked upon and touched with our hands, concerning the word of life . . . we proclaim also to you, so that you may have fellowship with us" (*1 Jn* 1:1, 3). *Jesus is the only Gospel:* we have nothing further to say or any other witness to bear.

To proclaim Jesus is itself to proclaim life. For Jesus is "the word of life" (*1 Jn* 1:1). In him "life was made manifest" (*1 Jn* 1:2); he himself is "the eternal life which was with the Father and was made manifest to us" (*1 Jn* 1:2). By the gift of the Spirit, this same life has been bestowed on us. It is in being destined to life in its fullness, to "eternal life", that every person's earthly life acquires its full meaning.

Enlightened by this *Gospel of life,* we feel a need to proclaim it and to bear witness to it in all its *marvellous newness.* Since it is one with Jesus himself, who makes all things new [103] and conquers the "oldness" which comes from sin and leads to death,[104] this Gospel exceeds every human expectation and reveals the sublime heights to which the dignity of the human person is raised through grace. This is how Saint Gregory of Nyssa understands it: "Man, as a being, is of no account; he is dust, grass, vanity. But once he is adopted by the God of the universe as a son, he becomes part of the family of that Being, whose excellence and greatness no one can see, hear or understand. What words, thoughts or flight of the spirit can praise the superabundance of this grace? Man surpasses his nature: mortal, he becomes immortal; perishable, he becomes imperishable; fleeting, he becomes eternal; human, he becomes divine".[105]

Gratitude and joy at the incomparable dignity of man impel us to share this message with everyone: "that which we have seen and heard we proclaim also to you, so that you may have fellowship with us" (*1 Jn* 1:3). We need to bring the *Gospel of life* to the heart of every man and woman and to make it penetrate every part of society.

81.   This involves above all proclaiming *the core* of this Gospel. It is the proclamation of a living God who is close to us, who calls us to profound communion with himself and awakens

in us the certain hope of eternal life. It is the affirmation of the inseparable connection between the person, his life and his bodiliness. It is the presentation of human life as a life of relationship, a gift of God, the fruit and sign of his love. It is the proclamation that Jesus has a unique relationship with every person, which enables us to see in every human face the face of Christ. It is the call for a "sincere gift of self" as the fullest way to realize our personal freedom.

It also involves making clear all *the consequences* of this Gospel. These can be summed up as follows: human life, as a gift of God, is sacred and inviolable. For this reason procured abortion and euthanasia are absolutely unacceptable. Not only must human life not be taken, but it must be protected with loving concern. The meaning of life is found in giving and receiving love, and in this light human sexuality and procreation reach their true and full significance. Love also gives meaning to suffering and death; despite the mystery which surrounds them, they can become saving events. Respect for life requires that science and technology should always be at the service of man and his integral development. Society as a whole must respect, defend and promote the dignity of every human person, at every moment and in every condition of that person's life.

82.   To be truly a people at the service of life we must propose these truths constantly and courageously from the very first proclamation of the Gospel, and thereafter *in catechesis, in the various forms of preaching, in personal dialogue and in all educational activity*. Teachers, catechists and theologians have the task of emphasizing the *anthropological reasons* upon which respect for every human life is based. In this way, by making the newness of the *Gospel of life* shine forth, we can also help everyone discover in the light of reason and of personal experience how the Christian message fully reveals what man is and the meaning of his being and existence. We shall find important points of contact and dialogue also with non-believers, in our common commitment to the establishment of a new culture of life.

Faced with so many opposing points of view, and a widespread rejection of sound doctrine concerning human life, we can feel that Paul's entreaty to Timothy is also addressed to us: "Preach the word, be urgent in season and out of season, convince, rebuke, and exhort, be unfailing in patience and in teaching" (*2 Tim* 4:2). This exhortation should resound with special force in the hearts of those members of the Church who directly share, in different ways, in her mission as "teacher" of the truth. May it resound above all for us who are *Bishops:* we are the first ones called to be untiring preachers of the *Gospel of life.* We are also entrusted with the task of ensuring that the doctrine which is once again being set forth in this Encyclical is faithfully handed on in its integrity. We must use appropriate means to defend the faithful from all teaching which is contrary to it. We need to make sure that in theological faculties, seminaries and Catholic institutions sound doctrine is taught, explained and more fully investigated.106 May Paul's exhortation strike a chord in all *theologians, pastors, teachers* and in all those responsible for *catechesis and the formation of consciences.* Aware of their specific role, may they never be so grievously irresponsible as to betray the truth and their own mission by proposing personal ideas contrary to the *Gospel of life* as faithfully presented and interpreted by the Magisterium.

In the proclamation of this Gospel, we must not fear hostility or unpopularity, and we must refuse any compromise or ambiguity which might conform us to the world's way of thinking (cf. *Rom* 12:2). We must be *in the world* but not *of the world* (cf. *Jn* 15:19; 17:16), drawing our strength from Christ, who by his Death and Resurrection has overcome the world (cf. *Jn* 16:33).

"I give you thanks, that I am, fearfully, wonder-fully made" (Ps 139:14): celebrating the Gospel of life

83.   Because we have been sent into the world as a "people for life", our proclamation must also become *a genuine celebration of the Gospel of life*. This celebration, with the evocative power of its gestures, symbols and rites, should become a precious and significant setting in which the beauty and grandeur of this Gospel is handed on.

For this to happen, we need first of all to *foster,* in ourselves and in others, *a contemplative outlook.*[107] Such an outlook arises from faith in the God of life, who has created every individual as a "wonder" (cf. *Ps* 139:14). It is the outlook of those who see life in its deeper meaning, who grasp its utter gratuitousness, its beauty and its invitation to freedom and responsibility. It is the outlook of those who do not presume to take pos-session of reality but instead accept it as a gift, discovering in all things the reflection of the Cre-ator and seeing in every person his living image (cf. *Gen* 1:27; *Ps* 8:5). This outlook does not give in to discouragement when confronted by those who are sick, suffering, outcast or at death's door. Instead, in all these situations it feels challenged to find meaning, and precisely in these circumstances it is open to perceiving in the face of every person a call to encounter, dialogue and solidarity.

It is time for all of us to adopt this outlook, and with deep religious awe to rediscover the ability to *revere and honour every person,* as Paul VI invited us to do in one of his first Christmas messages.[108] Inspired by this contemplative outlook, the new people of the redeemed cannot but respond with *songs of joy, praise and thanksgiving for the priceless gift of life,* for the mystery of every individual's call to share through Christ in the life of grace and in an existence of unending communion with God our Creator and Father.

84.   *To celebrate the Gospel of life means to celebrate the God of life, the God who gives life:* "We must celebrate Eternal Life, from which every other life proceeds. From this, in proportion to its capacities, every being which in any way participates in life, receives life. This Divine Life, which is above every other life, gives and preserves life. Every life and every living movement proceed from this Life which transcends all life and every principle of life. It is to this that souls owe their incorruptibility; and because of this all animals and plants live, which receive only

the faintest glimmer of life. To men, beings made of spirit and matter, Life grants life. Even if we should abandon Life, because of its overflowing love for man, it converts us and calls us back to itself. Not only this: it promises to bring us, soul and body, to perfect life, to immortality. It is too little to say that this Life is alive: it is the Principle of life, the Cause and sole Wellspring of life. Every living thing must contemplate it and give it praise: it is Life which overflows with life".[109]

Like the Psalmist, we too, in our *daily prayer* as individuals and as a community, praise and bless God our Father, who knitted us together in our mother's womb, and saw and loved us while we were still without form (cf. *Ps* 139:13, 15-16). We exclaim with overwhelming joy: "I give you thanks that I am fearfully, wonderfully made; wonderful are your works. You know me through and through" (*Ps* 139:14). Indeed, "despite its hardships, its hidden mysteries, its suffering and its inevitable frailty, this mortal life is a most beautiful thing, a marvel ever new and moving, an event worthy of being exalted in joy and glory".[110] Moreover, man and his life appear to us not only as one of the greatest marvels of creation: for God has granted to man a dignity which is near to divine (*Ps* 8:5-6). In every child which is born and in every person who lives or dies we

171

see the image of God's glory. We celebrate this glory in every human being, a sign of the living God, an icon of Jesus Christ.

We are called to express wonder and gratitude for the gift of life and to welcome, savour and share the Gospel of life not only in our personal and community prayer, but above all in the *celebrations of the liturgical year*. Particularly important in this regard are the *Sacraments,* the efficacious signs of the presence and saving action of the Lord Jesus in Christian life. The Sacraments make us sharers in divine life, and provide the spiritual strength necessary to experience life, suffering and death in their fullest meaning. Thanks to a genuine rediscovery and a better appreciation of the significance of these rites, our liturgical celebrations, especially celebrations of the Sacraments, will be ever more capable of expressing the full truth about birth, life, suffering and death, and will help us to live these moments as a participation in the Paschal Mystery of the Crucified and Risen Christ.

85.   In celebrating the *Gospel of life* we also need to *appreciate and make good use of the wealth of gestures and symbols present in the traditions and customs of different cultures and peoples*. There are special times and ways in which

the peoples of different nations and cultures express joy for a newborn life, respect for and protection of individual human lives, care for the suffering or needy, closeness to the elderly and the dying, participation in the sorrow of those who mourn, and hope and desire for immortality.

In view of this and following the suggestion made by the Cardinals in the Consistory of 1991, I propose that a *Day for Life* be celebrated each year in every country, as already established by some Episcopal Conferences. The celebration of this Day should be planned and carried out with the active participation of all sectors of the local Church. Its primary purpose should be to foster in individual consciences, in families, in the Church and in civil society a recognition of the meaning and value of human life at every stage and in every condition. Particular attention should be drawn to the seriousness of abortion and euthanasia, without neglecting other aspects of life which from time to time deserve to be given careful consideration, as occasion and circumstances demand.

86.   As part of the spiritual worship acceptable to God (cf. *Rom* 12:1), the *Gospel of life* is to be celebrated above all in *daily living,* which should be filled with self-giving love for others. In this

173

way, our lives will become a genuine and responsible acceptance of the gift of life and a heartfelt song of praise and gratitude to God who has given us this gift. This is already happening in the many different acts of selfless generosity, often humble and hidden, carried out by men and women, children and adults, the young and the old, the healthy and the sick.

It is in this context, so humanly rich and filled with love, that *heroic actions* too are born. These are *the most solemn celebration of the Gospel of life,* for they proclaim it *by the total gift of self.* They are the radiant manifestation of the highest degree of love, which is to give one's life for the person loved (cf. *Jn* 15:13). They are a sharing in the mystery of the Cross, in which Jesus reveals the value of every person, and how life attains its fullness in the sincere gift of self. Over and above such outstanding moments, there is an everyday heroism, made up of gestures of sharing, big or small, which build up an authentic culture of life. A particularly praiseworthy example of such gestures is the donation of organs, performed in an ethically acceptable manner, with a view to offering a chance of health and even of life itself to the sick who sometimes have no other hope.

Part of this daily heroism is also the silent but effective and eloquent witness of all those "brave mothers who devote themselves to their own family without reserve, who suffer in giving birth to their children and who are ready to make any effort, to face any sacrifice, in order to pass on to them the best of themselves".[111] In living out their mission "these heroic women do not always find support in the world around them. On the contrary, the cultural models frequently promoted and broadcast by the media do not encourage motherhood. In the name of progress and modernity the values of fidelity, chastity, sacrifice, to which a host of Christian wives and mothers have borne and continue to bear outstanding witness, are presented as obsolete . . . We thank you, heroic mothers, for your invincible love! We thank you for your intrepid trust in God and in his love. We thank you for the sacrifice of your life . . . In the Paschal Mystery, Christ restores to you the gift you gave him. Indeed, he has the power to give you back the life you gave him as an offering".[112]

"What does it profit, my brethren, if a man says he has faith but has not works?" (Jas 2:14): serving the Gospel of life

87.   By virtue of our sharing in Christ's royal mission, our support and promotion of human life must be accomplished through the *service of charity*, which finds expression in personal witness, various forms of volunteer work, social activity and political commitment. This is a *particularly pressing need at the present time,* when the "culture of death" so forcefully opposes the "culture of life" and often seems to have the upper hand. But even before that it is a need which springs from "faith working through love" (*Gal* 5:6). As the Letter of James admonishes us: "What does it profit, my brethren, if a man says he has faith but has not works? Can his faith save him? If a brother or sister is ill-clad and in lack of daily food, and one of you says to them, 'Go in peace, be warmed and filled', without giving them the things needed for the body, what does it profit? So faith by itself, if it has no works, is dead" (2:14-17).

In our service of charity, *we must be inspired and distinguished by a specific attitude:* we must care for the other as a person for whom God has made us responsible. As disciples of Jesus, we

176

are called to become neighbours to everyone (cf. *Lk* 10:29-37), and to show special favour to those who are poorest, most alone and most in need. In helping the hungry, the thirsty, the foreigner, the naked, the sick, the imprisoned—as well as the child in the womb and the old person who is suffering or near death—we have the opportunity to serve Jesus. He himself said: "As you did it to one of the least of these my brethren, you did it to me" (*Mt* 25:40). Hence we cannot but feel called to account and judged by the ever relevant words of Saint John Chrysostom: "Do you wish to honour the body of Christ? Do not neglect it when you find it naked. Do not do it homage here in the church with silk fabrics only to neglect it outside where it suffers cold and nakedness".[113]

Where life is involved, the *service of charity must be profoundly consistent.* It cannot tolerate bias and discrimination, for human life is sacred and inviolable at every stage and in every situation; it is an indivisible good. We need then to *"show care" for all life and for the life of everyone.* Indeed, at an even deeper level, we need to go to the very roots of life and love.

It is this deep love for every man and woman which has given rise down the centuries to an *outstanding history of charity,* a history which has brought into being in the Church and society many forms of service to life which evoke admiration from all unbiased observers. Every Christian community, with a renewed sense of responsibility, must continue to write this history through various kinds of pastoral and social activity. To this end, appropriate and effective programmes of *support for new life* must be implemented, with special closeness to mothers who, even without the help of the father, are not afraid to bring their child into the world and to raise it. Similar care must be shown for the life of the marginalized or suffering, especially in its final phases.

88.   All of this involves a patient and fearless *work of education* aimed at encouraging one and all to bear each other's burdens (cf. *Gal* 6:2). It requires a continuous promotion of *vocations to service,* particularly among the young. It involves the implementation of long-term practical *projects and initiatives* inspired by the Gospel.

Many are the *means* towards this end which *need to be developed* with skill and serious commitment. At the first stage of life, *centres for natural methods of regulating fertility* should be promoted as a valuable help to responsible parenthood, in which all individuals, and in the first place the child, are recognized and respected in their own right, and where every decision is guided by the ideal of the sincere gift of self. *Marriage and family counselling agencies* by their specific work of guidance and prevention, carried out in accordance with an anthropology consistent with the Christian vision of the person, of the couple and of sexuality, also offer valuable help in rediscovering the meaning of love and life, and in supporting and accompanying every family in its mission as the "sanctuary of life". Newborn life is also served by *centres of assistance and homes or centres where new life receives a welcome*. Thanks to the work of such centres, many unmarried mothers and couples in difficulty discover new hope and find assistance and support in overcoming hardship and the fear of accepting a newly conceived life or life which has just come into the world.

When life is challenged by conditions of hardship, maladjustment, sickness or rejection, other programmes—such as *communities for treating drug addiction, residential communities for minors or the mentally ill, care and relief centres for AIDS patients, associations for solidarity especially towards the disabled*—are eloquent expressions of what charity is able to devise in order to give everyone new reasons for hope and practical possibilities for life.

And when earthly existence draws to a close,

it is again charity which finds the most appropriate means for enabling the *elderly,* especially those who can no longer look after themselves, and the *terminally ill* to enjoy genuinely humane assistance and to receive an adequate response to their needs, in particular their anxiety and their loneliness. In these cases the role of families is indispensable; yet families can receive much help from social welfare agencies and, if necessary, from recourse to *palliative care,* taking advantage of suitable medical and social services available in public institutions or in the home.

In particular, the role of *hospitals, clinics* and *convalescent homes* needs to be reconsidered. These should not merely be institutions where care is provided for the sick or the dying. Above all they should be places where suffering, pain and death are acknowledged and understood in their human and specifically Christian meaning. This must be especially evident and effective in *institutes staffed by Religious or in any way connected with the Church.*

89.   Agencies and centres of service to life, and all other initiatives of support and solidarity which circumstances may from time to time suggest, need to be directed by *people who are generous in their involvement and fully aware* of the

importance of the *Gospel of life* for the good of individuals and society.

A unique responsibility belongs to health-care personnel: doctors, pharmacists, nurses, chaplains, men and women religious, administrators and volunteers. Their profession calls for them to be guardians and servants of human life. In today's cultural and social context, in which science and the practice of medicine risk losing sight of their inherent ethical dimension, health-care professionals can be strongly tempted at times to become manipulators of life, or even agents of death. In the face of this temptation their responsibility today is greatly increased. Its deepest inspiration and strongest support lie in the intrinsic and undeniable ethical dimension of the health-care profession, something already recognized by the ancient and still relevant *Hippocratic Oath,* which requires every doctor to commit himself to absolute respect for human life and its sacredness.

Absolute respect for every innocent human life also requires the *exercise of conscientious objection* in relation to procured abortion and euthanasia. "Causing death" can never be considered a form of medical treatment, even when the intention is solely to comply with the patient's request. Rather, it runs completely counter to the health-care profession, which is meant to be an impassioned and unflinching affirmation of life. Biomedical research too, a field which promises great benefits for humanity, must always reject experimentation, research or applications which disregard the inviolable dignity of the human being, and thus cease to be at the service of people and become instead means which, under the guise of helping people, actually harm them.

90.　　*Volunteer workers* have a specific role to play: they make a valuable contribution to the service of life when they combine professional ability and generous, selfless love. The *Gospel of life* inspires them to lift their feelings of good will towards others to the heights of Christ's charity; to renew every day, amid hard work and weariness, their awareness of the dignity of every person; to search out people's needs and, when necessary, to set out on new paths where needs are greater but care and support weaker.

If charity is to be realistic and effective, it demands that the *Gospel of life* be implemented also by means of certain *forms of social activity and commitment in the political field*, as a way of defending and promoting the value of life in our ever more complex and pluralistic societies. *Individuals, families, groups and associations*, albeit for different reasons and in different ways, all have a responsibility for shaping society and developing cultural, economic, political and legislative projects which, with respect for all and in keeping with democratic principles, will contribute to the building of a society in which the dignity of each person is recognized and protected and the lives of all are defended and enhanced.

This task is the particular responsibility of *civil leaders*. Called to serve the people and the common good, they have a duty to make courageous choices in support of life, especially through *legislative measures*. In a democratic system, where laws and decisions are made on the basis of the consensus of many, the sense of personal responsibility in the consciences of individuals invested with authority may be weakened. But no one can ever renounce this responsibility, especially when he or she has a legislative or decision-making mandate, which calls that person to answer to God, to his or her own conscience and to the whole of society for choices which may be contrary to the common good. Although laws are not the only means of protecting human life, nevertheless they do play a very important and sometimes decisive role in influencing patterns of thought and behaviour. I repeat once more that a law which violates an innocent person's natural right to life is unjust and, as such, is not valid as a law. For this reason I urgently appeal once more to all political leaders not to pass laws which, by disregarding the dignity of the person, undermine the very fabric of society.

The Church well knows that it is difficult to mount an effective legal defence of life in pluralistic democracies, because of the presence of strong cultural currents with differing outlooks. At the same time, certain that moral truth cannot fail to make its presence deeply felt in every conscience, the Church encourages political leaders, starting with those who are Christians, not to give in, but to make those choices which, taking into account what is realistically attainable, will lead to the reestablishment of a just order in the defence and promotion of the value of life. Here it must be noted that it is not enough to remove unjust laws. The underlying causes of attacks on life have to be eliminated, especially by ensuring proper support for families and motherhood. A *family policy must be the basis and driving force of all social policies*. For this reason there need to be set in place social and political initiatives capable of guaranteeing conditions of true freedom of choice in matters of parenthood. It is also necessary to rethink labour, urban, residential and social service policies so as to harmonize working schedules with time available for the family, so that it becomes effectively possible to take care of children and the elderly.

91.   Today an important part of policies which favour life is the *issue of population growth*. Certainly public authorities have a responsibility to "intervene to orient the demography of the population".[114] But such interventions must always take into account and respect the primary and inalienable responsibility of married couples and families, and cannot employ methods which fail to respect the person and fundamental human rights, beginning with the right to life of every innocent human being. It is therefore morally unacceptable to encourage, let alone impose, the use of methods such as contraception, sterilization and abortion in order to regulate births. The ways of solving the population problem are quite different. Governments and the various international agencies must above all strive to create economic, social, public health and cultural conditions which will enable married couples to make their choices about procreation in full freedom and with genuine responsibility. They must then make efforts to ensure "greater opportunities and a fairer distribution of wealth so that everyone can share equitably in the goods of

creation. Solutions must be sought on the global level by establishing a true *economy of communion and sharing of goods,* in both the national and international order".[115] This is the only way to respect the dignity of persons and families, as well as the authentic cultural patrimony of peoples.

Service of the *Gospel of life* is thus an immense and complex task. This service increasingly appears as a valuable and fruitful area for positive cooperation with our brothers and sisters of other Churches and ecclesial communities, in accordance with the *practical ecumenism* which the Second Vatican Council authoritatively encouraged.[116] It also appears as a providential area for dialogue and joint efforts with the followers of other religions and with all people of good will. *No single person or group has a monopoly on the defence and promotion of life. These are everyone's task and responsibility.* On the eve of the Third Millennium, the challenge facing us is an arduous one: only the concerted efforts of all those who believe in the value of life can prevent a setback of unforeseeable consequences for civilization.

186

"Your children will be like olive shoots around your table" (Ps 128:3): *the family as the "sanctuary of life"*

92.   Within the "people of life and the people for life", *the family has a decisive responsibility.* This responsibility flows from its very nature as a community of life and love, founded upon marriage, and from its mission to "guard, reveal and communicate love".[117] Here it is a matter of God's own love, of which parents are co-workers and as it were interpreters when they transmit life and raise it according to his fatherly plan.[118] This is the love that becomes selflessness, receptiveness and gift. Within the family each member is accepted, respected and honoured precisely because he or she is a person; and if any family member is in greater need, the care which he or she receives is all the more intense and attentive.

The family has a special role to play throughout the life of its members, from birth to death. It is truly "the *sanctuary of life:* the place in which life—the gift of God—can be properly welcomed and protected against the many attacks to which it is exposed, and can develop in accordance with what constitutes authentic human growth".[119] Consequently the role of the family in building a culture of life is *decisive and irreplaceable.*

As the *domestic church*, the family is summoned to proclaim, celebrate and serve the *Gospel of life*. This is a responsibility which first concerns married couples, called to be givers of life, on the basis of an ever greater *awareness of the meaning of procreation* as a unique event which clearly reveals that *human life is a gift received in order then to be given as a gift*. In giving origin to a new life, parents recognize that the child, "as the fruit of their mutual gift of love, is, in turn, a gift for both of them, a gift which flows from them".[120]

It is above all in *raising children* that the family fulfils its mission to proclaim the *Gospel of life*. By word and example, in the daily round of relations and choices, and through concrete actions and signs, parents lead their children to authentic freedom, actualized in the sincere gift of self, and they cultivate in them respect for others, a sense of justice, cordial openness, dialogue, generous service, solidarity and all the other values which help people to live life as a gift. In raising children Christian parents must be concerned about their children's faith and help them to fulfil the vocation God has given them. The parents' mission as educators also includes teaching and giving their children an example of the true meaning of suffering and death. They will be able to do this if they are sensitive to all kinds of suffering around them and, even more, if they succeed in fostering attitudes of closeness, assistance and sharing towards sick or elderly members of the family.

93.   The family *celebrates the Gospel of life* through *daily prayer*, both individual prayer and family prayer. The family prays in order to glorify and give thanks to God for the gift of life, and implores his light and strength in order to face times of difficulty and suffering without losing hope. But the celebration which gives meaning to every other form of prayer and worship is found in *the family's actual daily life together*, if it is a life of love and self-giving.

This celebration thus becomes a *service to the Gospel of life*, expressed through *solidarity* as experienced within and around the family in the form of concerned, attentive and loving care shown in the humble, ordinary events of each day. A particularly significant expression of solidarity between families is a willingness to *adopt* or *take in* children abandoned by their parents or in situations of serious hardship: True parental love is ready to go beyond the bonds of flesh and blood in order to accept children from other families, offering them whatever is necessary for their well-being and full development. Among the various forms of adoption, consideration should be given to *adoption-at-a-distance*, preferable in cases where the only reason for giving up the child is the extreme poverty of the child's family. Through this type of adoption, parents are given the help needed to support and raise their children, without their being uprooted from their natural environment.

As "a firm and persevering determination to commit oneself to the common good",[121] solidarity also needs to be practised through *participation in social and political life*. Serving the *Gospel of life* thus means that the family, particularly through its membership of family associations, works to ensure that the laws and institutions of the State in no way violate the right to life, from conception to natural death, but rather protect and promote it.

94.　　Special attention must be given to the *elderly*. While in some cultures older people remain a part of the family with an important and active role, in others the elderly are regarded as a useless burden and are left to themselves. Here the temptation to resort to euthanasia can more easily arise.

Neglect of the elderly or their outright rejection are intolerable. Their presence in the family, or at least their closeness to the family in cases where limited living space or other reasons make this impossible, is of fundamental importance in creating a climate of mutual interaction and enriching communication between the different age-groups. It is therefore important to preserve, or to re-establish where it has been lost, a sort of "covenant" between generations. In this way parents, in their later years, can receive from their children the acceptance and solidarity which they themselves gave to their children when they brought them into the world. This is required by obedience to the divine commandment to honour one's father and mother (cf. *Ex* 20:12; *Lev* 19:3). But there is more. The elderly are not only to be considered the object of our concern, closeness and service. They themselves have a valuable contribution to make to the *Gospel of life*. Thanks to the rich treasury of experiences they have acquired through the years, the elderly can and must *be sources of wisdom and witnesses of hope and love*.

Although it is true that "the future of humanity passes by way of the family",122 it must be admitted that modern social, economic and cultural conditions make the family's task of serving life more difficult and demanding. In order to fulfil its vocation as the "sanctuary of life", as the cell of a society which loves and welcomes life, *the family urgently needs to be helped and supported.* Communities and States must guarantee all the support, including economic support, which families need in order to meet their problems in a truly human way. For her part, the Church must untiringly promote a plan of pastoral care for families, capable of making every family rediscover and live with joy and courage its mission to further the *Gospel of life.*

"Walk as children of light" (*Eph* 5:8): *bringing about a transformation of culture*

95.   "Walk as children of light . . . and try to learn what is pleasing to the Lord. Take no part in the unfruitful works of darkness" (*Eph* 5:8, 10-11). In our present social context, marked by a dramatic struggle between the "culture of life" and the "culture of death", there is need to *develop a deep critical sense,* capable of discerning true values and authentic needs.

What is urgently called for is a *general mobilization of consciences* and a *united ethical effort* to activate a *great campaign in support of life. All together, we must build a new culture of life:* new, because it will be able to confront and solve to-day's unprecedented problems affecting human life; new, because it will be adopted with deeper and more dynamic conviction by all Christians; new, because it will be capable of bringing about a serious and courageous cultural dialogue among all parties. While the urgent need for such a cultural transformation is linked to the present historical situation, it is also rooted in the Church's mission of evangelization. The purpose of the Gospel, in fact, is "to transform humanity from within and to make it new".[123] Like the yeast which leavens the whole measure of dough (cf. *Mt* 13:33), the Gospel is meant to permeate all cultures and give them life from within,[124] so that they may express the full truth about the human person and about human life.

We need to begin with *the renewal of a culture of life within Christian communities themselves*. Too often it happens that believers, even those who take an active part in the life of the Church, end up by separating their Christian faith from its ethical requirements concerning life, and thus fall into moral subjectivism and certain objectionable ways of acting. With great openness and courage, we need to question how widespread is the culture of life today among individual Christians, families, groups and communities in our Dioceses. With equal clarity and determination we must identify the steps we are called to take in order to serve life in all its truth. At the same time, we need to promote a serious and in-depth exchange about basic issues of human life with everyone, including non-believers, in intellectual circles, in the various professional spheres and at the level of people's everyday life.

96.   The first and fundamental step towards this cultural transformation consists in *forming consciences* with regard to the incomparable and inviolable worth of every human life. It is of the greatest importance *to re-establish the essential connection between life and freedom.* These are inseparable goods: where one is violated, the other also ends up being violated. There is no true freedom where life is not welcomed and loved; and there is no fullness of life except in freedom. Both realities have something inherent and specific which links them inextricably: the vocation to love. Love, as a sincere gift of self,[125] is what gives the life and freedom of the person their truest meaning.

No less critical in the formation of conscience is *the recovery of the necessary link between freedom and truth.* As I have frequently stated, when freedom is detached from objective truth it becomes impossible to establish personal rights on a firm rational basis; and the ground is laid for society to be at the mercy of the unrestrained will of individuals or the oppressive totalitarianism of public authority.[126]

It is therefore essential that man should acknowledge his inherent condition as a creature to whom God has granted being and life as a gift and a duty. Only by admitting his innate dependence can man live and use his freedom to the full, and at the same time respect the life and freedom of every other person. Here especially one sees that "at the heart of every culture lies the attitude man takes to the greatest mystery: the mystery of God".[127] Where God is denied and people live as though he did not exist, or his commandments are not taken into account, the dignity of the human person and the inviolability of human life also end up being rejected or compromised.

97.   Closely connected with the formation of conscience is the *work of education,* which helps individuals to be ever more human, leads them ever more fully to the truth, instils in them growing respect for life, and trains them in right interpersonal relationships.

In particular, there is a need for education about the value of life *from its very origins.* It is an illusion to think that we can build a true culture of human life if we do not help the young to accept and experience sexuality and love and the whole of life according to their true meaning and in their close interconnection. Sexuality, which enriches the whole person, "manifests its inmost meaning in leading the person to the gift of self in love".[128] The trivialization of sexuality is among the principal factors which have led to contempt for new life. Only a true love is able to protect life. There can be no avoiding the duty to offer, especially to adolescents and young adults, an authentic *education in sexuality and in love,* an education which involves *training in chastity* as a virtue which fosters personal maturity and makes one capable of respecting the "spousal" meaning of the body.

The work of educating in the service of life involves the *training of married couples in responsible procreation.* In its true meaning, responsible procreation requires couples to be obedient to the Lord's call and to act as faithful interpreters of his plan. This happens when the family is generously open to new lives, and when couples maintain an attitude of openness and service to life, even if, for serious reasons and in respect for the moral law, they choose to avoid a new birth for the time being or indefinitely. The

196

moral law obliges them in every case to control the impulse of instinct and passion, and to respect the biological laws inscribed in their person. It is precisely this respect which makes legitimate, at the service of responsible procreation, the *use of natural methods of regulating fertility*. From the scientific point of view, these methods are becoming more and more accurate and make it possible in practice to make choices in harmony with moral values. An honest appraisal of their effectiveness should dispel certain prejudices which are still widely held, and should convince married couples, as well as health-care and social workers, of the importance of proper training in this area. The Church is grateful to those who, with personal sacrifice and often unacknowledged dedication, devote themselves to the study and spread of these methods, as well to the promotion of education in the moral values which they presuppose.

The work of education cannot avoid a consideration of suffering and death. These are a part of human existence, and it is futile, not to say misleading, to try to hide them or ignore them. On the contrary, people must be helped to understand their profound mystery in all its harsh reality. Even pain and suffering have meaning and value when they are experienced in close connection with love received and given. In this regard, I have called for the yearly celebration of the *World Day of the Sick,* emphasizing "the salvific nature of the offering up of suffering which, experienced in communion with Christ, belongs to the very essence of the Redemption".[129] Death itself is anything but an event without hope. It is the door which opens wide on eternity and, for those who live in Christ, an experience of participation in the mystery of his Death and Resurrection.

98.   In a word, we can say that the cultural change which we are calling for demands from everyone the courage to *adopt a new life-style,* consisting in making practical choices—at the personal, family, social and international level— on the basis of a correct scale of values: *the primacy of being over having,*[130] *of the person over things.*[131] This renewed life-style involves a passing from *indifference to concern for others, from rejection to acceptance of them.* Other people are not rivals from whom we must defend ourselves, but brothers and sisters to be supported. They are to be loved for their own sakes, and they enrich us by their very presence.

In this mobilization for a new culture of life no one must feel excluded: *everyone has an important role to play.* Together with the family, *teachers* and *educators* have a particularly valuable contribution to make. Much will depend on them if young people, trained in true freedom, are to be able to preserve for themselves and make known to others new, authentic ideals of life, and if they are to grow in respect for and service to every other person, in the family and in society.

Intellectuals can also do much to build a new culture of human life. A special task falls to *Catholic* intellectuals, who are called to be present and active in the leading centres where culture is formed, in schools and universities, in places of scientific and technological research, of artistic creativity and of the study of man. Allowing their talents and activity to be nourished by the living force of the Gospel, they ought to place themselves at the service of a new culture of life by offering serious and well documented contributions, capable of commanding general respect and interest by reason of their merit. It was precisely for this purpose that I established the *Pontifical Academy for Life,* assigning it the task of "studying and providing information and training about the principal problems of law and biomedicine pertaining to the promotion of life, especially in the direct relationship they have with Christian morality and the directives of the Church's Magisterium".132 A specific contribution will also have to come from *Universities,* particularly from *Catholic* Universities, and from *Centres, Institutes and Committees of Bioethics.*

An important and serious responsibility belongs to *those involved in the mass media,* who are called to ensure that the messages which they so effectively transmit will support the culture of life. They need to present noble models of life and make room for instances of people's positive and sometimes heroic love for others. With great respect they should also present the positive values of sexuality and human love, and not insist on what defiles and cheapens human dignity. In their interpretation of things, they should refrain from emphasizing anything that suggests or fosters feelings or attitudes of indifference, contempt or rejection in relation to life. With scrupulous concern for factual truth, they are called to combine freedom of information with respect for every person and a profound sense of humanity.

99.   In transforming culture so that it supports life, *women* occupy a place, in thought and action, which is unique and decisive. It depends on them to promote a "new feminism" which rejects the temptation of imitating models of "male domination", in order to acknowledge and affirm the true genius of women in every aspect of the life

200

of society, and overcome all discrimination, violence and exploitation.

Making my own the words of the concluding message of the Second Vatican Council, I address to women this urgent appeal: *"Reconcile people with life"*.133 You are called to *bear witness to the meaning of genuine love,* of that gift of self and of that acceptance of others which are present in a special way in the relationship of husband and wife, but which ought also to be at the heart of every other interpersonal relationship. The experience of motherhood makes you acutely aware of the other person and, at the same time, confers on you a particular task: "Motherhood involves a special communion with the mystery of life, as it develops in the woman's womb . . . This unique contact with the new human being developing within her gives rise to an attitude towards human beings not only towards her own child, but every human being, which profoundly marks the woman's personality".134 A mother welcomes and carries in her self another human being, enabling it to grow inside her, giving it room, respecting it in its otherness. Women first learn and then teach others that human relations are authentic if they are open to accepting the other person: a person who is recognized and loved because of the dignity which comes from being a

201

person and not from other considerations, such as usefulness, strength, intelligence, beauty or health. This is the fundamental contribution which the Church and humanity expect from women. And it is the indispensable prerequisite for an authentic cultural change.

I would now like to say a special word to *women who have had an abortion.* The Church is aware of the many factors which may have influenced your decision, and she does not doubt that in many cases it was a painful and even shattering decision. The wound in your heart may not yet have healed. Certainly what happened was and remains terribly wrong. But do not give in to discouragement and do not lose hope. Try rather to understand what happened and face it honestly. If you have not already done so, give yourselves over with humility and trust to repentance. The Father of mercies is ready to give you his forgiveness and his peace in the Sacrament of Reconciliation. You will come to understand that nothing is definitively lost and you will also be able to ask forgiveness from your child, who is now living in the Lord. With the friendly and expert help and advice of other people, and as a result of your own painful experience, you can be among the most eloquent defenders of everyone's right to life. Through your commitment to life, whether by accepting the birth of other children or by welcoming and caring for those most in need of someone to be close to them, you will become promoters of a new way of looking at human life.

100.   In this great endeavour to create a new culture of life we are *inspired and sustained by the confidence* that comes from knowing that the *Gospel of life,* like the Kingdom of God itself, is growing and producing abundant fruit (cf. *Mk* 4:26-29). There is certainly an enormous disparity between the powerful resources available to the forces promoting the "culture of death" and the means at the disposal of those working for a "culture of life and love". But we know that we can rely on the help of God, for whom nothing is impossible (cf. *Mt* 19:26).

Filled with this certainty, and moved by profound concern for the destiny of every man and woman, I repeat what I said to those families who carry out their challenging mission amid so many difficulties:[135] *a great prayer for life is urgently needed,* a prayer which will rise up throughout the world. Through special initiatives and in daily prayer, may an impassioned plea rise to God, the Creator and lover of life, from every Christian community, from every group and association, from every family and from the heart of every believer. Jesus himself has shown us by his own example that prayer and fasting are the first and most effective weapons against the forces of evil (cf. *Mt* 4:1-11). As he taught his disciples, some demons cannot be driven out except in this way (cf. *Mk* 9:29). Let us therefore discover anew the humility and the courage to *pray and fast* so that power from on high will break down the walls of lies and deceit: the walls which conceal from the sight of so many of our brothers and sisters the evil of practices and laws which are hostile to life. May this same power turn their hearts to resolutions and goals inspired by the civilization of life and love.

"We are writing this that our joy may be complete" (*1 Jn* 1:4): *the Gospel of life is for the whole of human society*

101.   "We are writing you this that our joy may be complete" (*1 Jn* 1:4). The revelation of the *Gospel of life* is given to us as a good to be shared with all people: so that all men and women may have fellowship with us and with the Trinity (cf. *1 Jn* 1:3). Our own joy would not be complete if we failed to share this Gospel with others but kept it only for ourselves.

   The Gospel of life is not for believers alone:

it is for everyone. The issue of life and its defence and promotion is not a concern of Christians alone. Although faith provides special light and strength, this question arises in every human conscience which seeks the truth and which cares about the future of humanity. Life certainly has a sacred and religious value, but in no way is that value a concern only of believers. The value at stake is one which every human being can grasp by the light of reason; thus it necessarily concerns everyone.

Consequently, all that we do as the "people of life and for life" should be interpreted correctly and welcomed with favour. When the Church declares that unconditional respect for the right to life of every innocent person—from conception to natural death—is one of the pillars on which every civil society stands, she "wants simply *to promote a human State. A State* which recognizes the defence of the fundamental rights of the human person, especially of the weakest, as its primary duty".[136]

The Gospel of life is for the whole of human society. To be actively pro-life is to contribute to the *renewal of society* through the promotion of the common good. It is impossible to further the common good without acknowledging and defending the right to life, upon which all the other inalienable rights of individuals are founded and from which they develop. A society lacks solid foundations when, on the one hand, it asserts values such as the dignity of the person, justice and peace, but then, on the other hand, radically acts to the contrary by allowing or tolerating a variety of ways in which human life is devalued and violated, especially where it is weak or marginalized. Only respect for life can be the foundation and guarantee of the most precious and essential goods of society, such as democracy and peace.

There can be no *true democracy* without a recognition of every person's dignity and without respect for his or her rights.

Nor can there be *true peace* unless *life is defended and promoted*. As Paul VI pointed out: "Every crime against life is an attack on peace, especially if it strikes at the moral conduct of people . . . But where human rights are truly professed and publicly recognized and defended, peace becomes the joyful and operative climate of life in society".[137]

The "people of life" rejoices in being able to share its commitment with so many others. Thus may the "people for life" constantly grow in number and may a new culture of love and solidarity develop for the true good of the whole of human society.

CONCLUSION

102.   At the end of this Encyclical, we naturally look again to the Lord Jesus, "the Child born for us" (cf. *Is* 9:6), that in him we may contemplate "the Life" which "was made manifest" (*1 Jn* 1:2). In the mystery of Christ's Birth the encounter of God with man takes place and the earthly journey of the Son of God begins, a journey which will culminate in the gift of his life on the Cross. By his death Christ will conquer death and become for all humanity the source of new life.

The one who accepted "Life" in the name of all and for the sake of all was Mary, the Virgin Mother; she is thus most closely and personally associated with the *Gospel of life*. Mary's consent at the Annunciation and her motherhood stand at the very beginning of the mystery of life which Christ came to bestow on humanity (cf. *Jn* 10:10). Through her acceptance and loving care for the life of the Incarnate Word, human life has been rescued from condemnation to final and eternal death.

For this reason, Mary, "like the Church of which she is the type, is a mother of all who are reborn to life. She is in fact the mother of the Life by which everyone lives, and when she brought it forth from herself she in some way brought to rebirth all those who were to live by that Life".[138]

As the Church contemplates Mary's motherhood, she discovers the meaning of her own motherhood and the way in which she is called to express it. At the same time, the Church's experience of motherhood leads to a most profound understanding of Mary's experience as the *incomparable model of how life should be welcomed and cared for.*

"A great portent appeared in heaven, a woman clothed with the sun" (Rev 12:1): the motherhood of Mary and of the Church

103.   The mutual relationship between the mystery of the Church and Mary appears clearly in the "great portent" described in the Book of Revelation: "A great portent appeared in heaven, a woman clothed with the sun, with the moon under her feet, and on her head a crown of twelve stars" (12:1). In this sign the Church recognizes an image of her own mystery: present in history,

she knows that she transcends history, inasmuch as she constitutes on earth the "seed and beginning" of the Kingdom of God.[139] The Church sees this mystery fulfilled in complete and exemplary fashion in Mary. She is the woman of glory in whom God's plan could be carried out with supreme perfection.

The "woman clothed with the sun"—the Book of Revelation tells us—"was with child" (12:2). The Church is fully aware that she bears within herself the Saviour of the world, Christ the Lord. She is aware that she is called to offer Christ to the world, giving men and women new birth into God's own life. But the Church cannot forget that her mission was made possible by the motherhood of Mary, who conceived and bore the One who is "God from God", "true God from true God". Mary is truly the Mother of God, the *Theotokos,* in whose motherhood the vocation to motherhood bestowed by God on every woman is raised to its highest level. Thus Mary becomes the model of the Church, called to be the "new Eve", the mother of believers, the mother of the "living" (cf. *Gen* 3:20).

The Church's spiritual motherhood is only achieved—the Church knows this too—through the pangs and "the labour" of childbirth (cf. *Rev* 12:2), that is to say, in constant tension with the forces of evil which still roam the world and affect human hearts, offering resistance to Christ: "In him was life, and the life was the light of men. The light shines in the darkness, and the darkness has not overcome it" (*Jn* 1:4-5).

Like the Church, Mary too had to live her motherhood amid suffering: "This child is set . . . for a sign that is spoken against—and a sword will pierce through your own soul also—that thoughts out of many hearts may be revealed" (*Lk* 2:34-35). The words which Simeon addresses to Mary at the very beginning of the Saviour's earthly life sum up and prefigure the rejection of Jesus, and with him of Mary, a rejection which will reach its culmination on Calvary. "Standing by the cross of Jesus" (*Jn* 19:25), Mary shares in the gift which the Son makes of himself: she offers Jesus, gives him over, and begets him to the end for our sake. The "yes" spoken on the day of the Annunciation reaches full maturity on the day of the Cross, when the time comes for Mary to receive and beget as her children all those who become disciples, pouring out upon them the saving love of her Son: "When Jesus saw his mother, and the disciple whom he loved standing near, he said to his mother, 'Woman, behold, your son!' " (*Jn* 19:26).

"And the dragon stood before the woman . . . that he might devour her child when she brought it forth" (Rev 12:4): life menaced by the forces of evil

104.   In the Book of Revelation, the "great portent" of the "woman" (12:1) is accompanied by "another portent which appeared in heaven": "a great red dragon" (*Rev* 12:3), which represents Satan, the personal power of evil, as well as all the powers of evil at work in history and opposing the Church's mission.

Here too Mary sheds light on the Community of Believers. The hostility of the powers of evil is, in fact, an insidious opposition which, before affecting the disciples of Jesus, is directed against his mother. To save the life of her Son from those who fear him as a dangerous threat, Mary has to flee with Joseph and the Child into Egypt (cf. *Mt* 2:13-15).

Mary thus helps the Church to *realize that life is always at the centre of a great struggle* between good and evil, between light and darkness. The dragon wishes to devour "the child brought forth" (cf. *Rev* 12:4), a figure of Christ, whom Mary brought forth "in the fullness of time" (*Gal* 4:4) and whom the Church must unceasingly offer to people in every age. But in a way that child is also a figure of every person, every child, especially every helpless baby whose life is threatened, because—as the Council reminds us—"by his Incarnation the Son of God has united himself in some fashion with every person".[140] It is precisely in the "flesh" of every person that Christ continues to reveal himself and to enter into fellowship with us, so that *rejection of human life,* in whatever form that rejection takes, *is really a rejection of Christ.* This is the fascinating but also demanding truth which Christ reveals to us and which his Church continues untiringly to proclaim: "Whoever receives one such child in my name receives me" (*Mt* 18:5); "Truly, I say to you, as you did it to one of the least of these my brethren, you did it to me" (*Mt* 25 :40).

"Death shall be no more" (Rev 21:4): the splendour of the Resurrection

105.   The angel's Annunciation to Mary is framed by these reassuring words: "Do not be afraid, Mary" and "with God nothing will be impossible" (*Lk* 1:30, 37). The whole of the Virgin Mother's life is in fact pervaded by the certainty

that God is near to her and that he accompanies her with his providential care. The same is true of the Church, which finds "a place prepared by God" (*Rev* 12:6) in the desert, the place of trial but also of the manifestation of God's love for his people (cf. *Hos* 2:16). Mary is a living word of comfort for the Church in her struggle against death. Showing us the Son, the Church assures us that in him the forces of death have already been defeated: "Death with life contended: combat strangely ended! Life's own Champion, slain, yet lives to reign".[141]

The Lamb who was slain is alive, bearing the marks of his Passion in the splendour of the Resurrection. He alone is master of all the events of history: he opens its "seals" (cf. *Rev* 5:1-10) and proclaims, in time and beyond, *the power of life over death.* In the "new Jerusalem", that new world towards which human history is travelling, *"death shall be no more,* neither shall there be mourning nor crying nor pain any more, for the former things have passed away" (*Rev* 21:4).

And as we, the pilgrim people, the people of life and for life, make our way in confidence towards "a new heaven and a new earth" (*Rev* 21:1), we look to her who is for us "a sign of sure hope and solace".[142]

O Mary,
bright dawn of the new world,
Mother of the living,
to you do we entrust the *cause of life:*
Look down, O Mother,
upon the vast numbers
of babies not allowed to be born
of the poor whose lives are made difficult,
of men and women
who are victims of brutal violence,
of the elderly and the sick killed
by indifference or out of misguided mercy.
Grant that all who believe in your Son
may *proclaim the Gospel of life*
with honesty and love
to the people of our time.
Obtain for them the grace
to *accept that Gospel*
as a gift ever new,
the joy *of celebrating* it with gratitude
throughout their lives
and the courage to *bear witness to it*
resolutely, in order to build,
together with all people of good will,
the civilization of truth and love,
to the praise and glory of God,
the Creator and lover of life.

Given in Rome, at Saint Peter's, on 25 March, the Solemnity of the Annunciation of the Lord, in the year 1995, the seventeenth of my Pontificate.

Joannes Paulus II

NOTES

1. The expression "Gospel of life" is not found as such in Sacred Scripture. But it does correspond to an essential dimension of the biblical message.

2. Pastoral Constitution on the Church in the Modern World *Gaudium et Spes,* 22.

3. Cf. JOHN PAUL II, Encyclical Letter *Redemptor Hominis* (4 March 1979), 10: *AAS* 71 (1979), 275.

4. Cf. *ibid.,* 14: *loc. cit.,* 285.

5. Pastoral Constitution on the Church in the Modern World *Gaudium et Spes,* 27.

6. Cf. Letter to all my Brothers in the Episcopate regarding the "Gospel of Life" (19 May 1991): *Insegnamenti* XIV, 1 (1991), 1293-1296.

7. *Ibid., loc. cit.,* p. 1294.

8. Letter to Families *Gratissimam sane* (2 February 1994), 4: *AAS* 86 (1994), 871.

9. JOHN PAUL II, Encyclical Letter *Centesimus Annus* (1 May 1991), 39: *AAS* 83 (1991), 842.

10. No. 2259.

11. Cf. SAINT AMBROSE, *De Noe,* 26:94-96: *CSEL* 32, 480-481.

12. Cf. *Catechism of the Catholic Church,* Nos. 1867 and 2268.

13. *De Cain et Abel,* II, 10, 38: *CSEL,* 32, 408.

14. Cf. CONGREGATION FOR THE DOCTRINE OF THE FAITH, Instruction on Respect for Human Life in

its Origin and on the Dignity of Procreation *Donum Vitae: AAS* 80 (1988), 70-102.

15. Address during the Prayer Vigil for the Eighth World Youth Day, Denver, 14 August 1993, II, 3: *AAS* 86 (1994), 419.

16. JOHN PAUL II, Address to the Participants at the Study Conference on "The Right to Life and Europe", 18 December 1987: *Insegnamenti,* X, 3 (1987), 1446-1447.

17. Pastoral Constitution on the Church in the Modern World *Gaudium et Spes,* 36.

18. Cf. *ibid.,* 16.

19. Cf. SAINT GREGORY THE GREAT, *Moralia in Job,* 13, 23: *CCL* 143A, 683.

20. JOHN PAUL II, Encyclical Letter *Redemptor Hominis* (4 March 1979), 10: *AAS* 71 (1979), 274.

21. SECOND VATICAN ECUMENICAL COUNCIL, Pastoral Constitution on the Church in the Modern World *Gaudium et Spes,* 50.

22. Dogmatic Constitution on Divine Revelation *Dei Verbum,* 4.

23. "Gloria Dei vivens homo": *Adversus Haereses,* IV, 20, 7: *SCh* 100/2, 648-649.

24. SECOND VATICAN ECUMENICAL COUNCIL, Pastoral Constitution on the Church in the Modern World *Gaudium et Spes,* 12.

25. *Confessions,* I, 1: *CCL* 27, 1.

26. *Exameron,* VI, 75-76: *CSEL* 32, 260-261.

27. "Vita autem hominis visio Dei": *Adversus Haereses,* IV, 20, 7: *SCh* 100/2, 648-649.

28. Cf. JOHN PAUL II, Encyclical Letter *Centesimus Annus* (1 May 1991), 38: *AAS* 83 (1991), 840-841.

29. JOHN PAUL II, Encyclical Letter *Sollicitudo*

Rei Socialis (30 December 1987), 34: *AAS* 80 (1988), 560.

30. Pastoral Constitution on the Church in the Modern World *Gaudium et Spes,* 50.

31. Letter to Families *Gratissimam sane* (2 February 1994), 9: *AAS* 86 (1994), 878; cf. PIUS XII, Encyclical Letter *Humani Generis* (12 August 1950): *AAS* 42 (1950), 574.

32. "Animas enim a Deo immediate creari catholica fides nos retinere iubet": PIUS XII, Encyclical Letter *Humani Generis* (12 August 1950): *AAS* 42 (1950), 575.

33. SECOND VATICAN ECUMENICAL COUNCIL, Pastoral Constitution on the Church in the Modern World *Gaudium et Spes,* 50; cf. JOHN PAUL II, Post-Synodal Apostolic Exhortation *Familiaris Consortio* (22 November 1981), 28: *AAS* 74 (1982), 114.

34. *Homilies,* II, 1: *CCSG* 3, 39.

35. See, for example, Psalms 22:10-11; 71:6; 139:13-14.

36. *Expositio Evangelii secundum Lucam,* II, 22-23: *CCL,* 14, 40-41.

37. SAINT IGNATIUS OF ANTIOCH, *Letter to the Ephesians,* 7, 2: *Patres Apostolici,* ed. F.X. Funk, II, 82.

38. *De Hominis Opificio,* 4: *PG* 44, 136.

39. Cf. SAINT JOHN DAMASCENE, *De Fide Orthodoxa,* 2, 12: *PG* 94, 920.922, quoted in SAINT THOMAS AQUINAS, *Summa Theologiae,* I-II, Prologue.

40. PAUL VI, Encyclical Letter *Humanae Vitae* (25 July 1968), 13: *AAS* 60 (1968), 489.

41. CONGREGATION FOR THE DOCTRINE OF THE

FAITH, Instruction on Respect for Human Life in its Origin and on the Dignity of Procreation *Donum Vitae* (22 February 1987), Introduction, No. 5: *AAS* 80 (1988), 76-77; cf. *Catechism of the Catholic Church,* No. 2258.

42. *Didache,* I, 1; II, 1-2; V, 1 and 3: *Patres Apostolici,* ed. F.X. Funk, I, 2-3, 6-9, 14-17; cf. *Letter of Pseudo-Barnabas,* XIX, 5: *loc. cit.,* 90-93.

43. Cf. *Catechism of the Catholic Church,* Nos. 2263-2269; cf. also *Catechism of the Council of Trent* III, §§ 327-332.

44. *Catechism of the Catholic Church,* No. 2265.

45. Cf. SAINT THOMAS AQUINAS, *Summa Theologiae,* II-II, q. 64, a. 7; SAINT ALPHONSUS DE' LIGUORI, *Theologia Moralis,* l. III, tr. 4, c. 1, dub. 3.

46. *Catechism of the Catholic Church,* No. 2266.

47. Cf. *ibid.*

48. No. 2267.

49. SECOND VATICAN ECUMENICAL COUNCIL, Dogmatic Constitution on the Church *Lumen Gentium,* 12.

50. Cf. SECOND VATICAN ECUMENICAL COUNCIL, Pastoral Constitution on the Church in the Modern World *Gaudium et Spes,* 27.

51. Cf. SECOND VATICAN ECUMENICAL COUNCIL, Dogmatic Constitution on the Church *Lumen Gentium,* 25.

52. CONGREGATION FOR THE DOCTRINE OF THE FAITH, Declaration on Euthanasia *Iura et Bona* (5 May 1980), II: *AAS* 72 (1980), 546.

53. JOHN PAUL II, Encyclical Letter *Veritatis Splendor* (6 August 1993), 96: *AAS* 85 (1993), 1209.

54. Pastoral Constitution on the Church in the

Modern World *Gaudium et Spes,* 51: "Abortus nec-non infanticidium nefanda sunt crimina".

55. Cf. JOHN PAUL II, Apostolic Letter *Mulieris Dignitatem* (15 August 1988), 14: *AAS* 80 (1988), 1686.

56. No. 21: *AAS* 86 (1994), 920.

57. CONGREGATION FOR THE DOCTRINE OF THE FAITH, *Declaration on Procured Abortion* (18 November 1974), Nos. 12-13: *AAS* 66 (1974), 738.

58. CONGREGATION FOR THE DOCTRINE OF THE FAITH, Instruction on Respect for Human Life in its Origin and on the Dignity of Procreation *Donum Vitae* (22 February 1987), I, No. 1: *AAS* 80 (1988), 78-79.

59. *Ibid., loc. cit.,* 79.

60. Hence the Prophet Jeremiah: "The word of the Lord came to me saying: 'Before I formed you in the womb I knew you, and before you were born I consecrated you; I appointed you a prophet to the nations' " (1:4-5). The Psalmist, for his part, addresses the Lord in these words: "Upon you I have leaned from my birth; you are he who took me from my mother's womb" (*Ps* 71:6; cf. *Is* 46:3; *Job* 10:8-12; *Ps* 22:10-11). So too the Evangelist Luke—in the magnificent episode of the meeting of the two mothers, Elizabeth and Mary, and their two sons, John the Baptist and Jesus, still hidden in their mothers' wombs (cf. 1:39-45)—emphasizes how even before their birth the two little ones are able to communicate: the child recognizes the coming of the Child and leaps for joy.

61. Cf. *Declaration on Procured Abortion* (18 November 1974), No. 7: *AAS* 66 (1974), 740-747.

62. "You shall not kill a child by abortion nor shall you kill it once it is born": V, 2: *Patres Apostolici,* ed. F.X. Funk, I, 17.

63. *Apologia on behalf of the Christians,* 35: *PG* 6, 969.

64. *Apologeticum,* IX, 8: *CSEL* 69, 24.

65. Cf. Encyclical Letter *Casti Connubii* (31 December 1930), II: *AAS* 22 (1930), 562-592.

66. Address to the Biomedical Association "San Luca" (12 November 1944): *Discorsi e Radiomessaggi,* VI (1944-1945), 191; cf. Address to the Italian Catholic Union of Midwives (29 October 1951), No. 2: *AAS* 43 (1951), 838.

67. Encyclical Letter *Mater et Magistra* (15 May 1961), 3: *AAS* 53 (1961), 447.

68. Pastoral Constitution on the Church in the Modern World *Gaudium et Spes,* 51.

69. Canon 2350, § 1.

70. *Code of Canon Law,* canon 1398; cf. *Code of Canons of the Eastern Churches,* canon 1450, § 2.

71. Cf. *ibid.,* canon 1329; also *Code of Canons of the Eastern Churches,* canon 1417.

72. Cf. Address to the National Congress of Italian Jurists (9 December 1972): *AAS* 64 (1972), 777; Encyclical Letter *Humanae Vitae* (25 July 1968), 14: *AAS* 60 (1968), 490.

73. Cf. Second Vatican Ecumenical Council, Dogmatic Constitution on the Church *Lumen Gentium,* 25.

74. Congregation for the Doctrine of the Faith, Instruction on Respect for Human Life in its Origin and on the Dignity of Procreation *Donum Vitae* (22 February 1987) I, 3: *AAS* 80 (1988), 80.

75. *Charter of the Rights of the Family* (22 October 1983), article 4b: Vatican Polyglot Press, 1983.

76. Congregation for the Doctrine of the

FAITH, Declaration on Euthanasia *Iura et Bona* (5 May 1980), II: *AAS* 72 (1980), 546.

77. *Ibid.,* IV: *loc. cit.,* 551.

78. Cf. *ibid.*

79. PIUS XII, Address to an International Group of Physicians (24 February 1957), III: *AAS* 49 (1957), 147; cf. CONGREGATION FOR THE DOCTRINE OF THE FAITH, Declaration on Euthanasia *Iura et Bona,* III: *AAS* 72 (1980), 547-548.

80. PIUS XII, Address to an International Group of Physicians (24 February 1957), III: *AAS* 49 (1957), 145.

81. Cf. PIUS XII, Address to an International Group of Physicians (24 February 1957): *loc. cit.,* 129-147; CONGREGATION OF THE HOLY OFFICE, *Decretum de directa insontium occisione* (2 December 1940): *AAS* 32 (1940), 553-554; PAUL VI, Message to French Television: "Every life is sacred" (27 January 1971): *Insegnamenti* IX (1971), 57-58; Address to the International College of Surgeons (1 June 1972): *AAS* 64 (1972), 432-436; SECOND VATICAN ECUMENICAL COUNCIL, Pastoral Constitution on the Church in the Modern World *Gaudium et Spes,* 27.

82. Cf. SECOND VATICAN ECUMENICAL COUNCIL, Dogmatic Constitution on the Church *Lumen Gentium,* 25.

83. Cf. SAINT AUGUSTINE, *De Civitate Dei* I, 20: *CCL* 47, 22; SAINT THOMAS AQUINAS, *Summa Theologiae,* II-II, q. 6, a. 5.

84. CONGREGATION FOR THE DOCTRINE OF THE FAITH, Declaration on Euthanasia *Iura et Bona* (5 May 1980), I: *AAS* 72 (1980), 545; *Catechism of the Catholic Church,* Nos. 2281-2283.

85. *Ep.* 204, 5: *CSEL* 57, 320.

86. Pastoral Constitution on the Church in the Modern World *Gaudium et Spes,* 18.

87. Cf. JOHN PAUL II, Apostolic Letter *Salvifici Doloris* (11 February 1984), 14-24: *AAS* 76 (1984), 214-234.

88. Cf. JOHN PAUL II, Encyclical Letter *Centesimus Annus* (1 May 1991), 46: *AAS* 83 (1991), 850; PIUS XII, Christmas Radio Message (24 December 1944): *AAS* 37 (1945), 10-20.

89. Cf. JOHN PAUL II, Encyclical Letter *Veritatis Splendor* (6 August 1993), 97 and 99: *AAS* 85 (1993), 1209-1211.

90. CONGREGATION FOR THE DOCTRINE OF THE FAITH, Instruction on Respect for Life in its Origin and on the Dignity of Procreation *Donum Vitae* (22 February 1987), III: *AAS* 80 (1988), 98.

91. Cf. SECOND VATICAN ECUMENICAL COUNCIL, Declaration on Religious Freedom *Dignitatis Humanae,* 7.

92. Cf. SAINT THOMAS AQUINAS, *Summa Theologiae* I-II, q. 96, a. 2.

93. Cf. SECOND VATICAN ECUMENICAL COUNCIL, Declaration on Religious Freedom *Dignitatis Humanae,* 7.

94. Encyclical Letter *Pacem in Terris* (11 April 1963), II: *AAS* 55 (1963), 273-274. The internal quote is from PIUS XII, Radio Message of Pentecost 1941 (1 June 1941): *AAS* 33 (1941), 200. On this topic, the Encyclical cites: PIUS XI, Encyclical Letter *Mit brennender Sorge* (14 March 1937): *AAS* 29 (1937), 159; Encyclical Letter *Divini Redemptoris* (19 March 1937), III: *AAS* 29 (1937), 79; PIUS XII, Christmas

Radio Message (24 December 1942): *AAS* 35 (1943), 9-24.

95. Encyclical Letter *Pacem in Terris* (11 April 1963), II: *loc. cit.*, 271.

96. *Summa Theologiae*, I-II, q. 93, a. 3, ad 2um.

97. *Ibid.*, I-II, q. 95, a. 2. Aquinas quotes SAINT AUGUSTINE: "Non videtur esse lex, quae iusta non fuerit", *De Libero Arbitrio,* I, 5, 11: *PL* 32, 1227.

98. CONGREGATION FOR THE DOCTRINE OF THE FAITH, *Declaration on Procured Abortion* (18 November 1974), No. 22: *AAS* 66 (1974), 744.

99. Cf. *Catechism of the Catholic Church,* Nos. 1753-1755; JOHN PAUL II, Encyclical Letter *Veritatis Splendor* (6 August 1993), 81-82: *AAS* 85 (1993), 1198-1199.

100. *In Iohannis Evangelium Tractatus,* 41, 10: *CCL* 36, 363; cf. JOHN PAUL II, Encyclical Letter *Veritatis Splendor* (6 August 1993), 13: *AAS* 85 (1993), 1144.

101. Apostolic Exhortation *Evangelii Nuntiandi* (8 December 1975), 14: *AAS* 68 (1976), 13.

102. Cf. *Roman Missal,* prayer of the celebrant before communion.

103. Cf. SAINT IRENAEUS: "Omnem novitatem attulit, semetipsum afferens, qui fuerat annuntiatus", *Adversus Haereses:* IV, 34, 1: *SCh* 100/2, 846-847.

104. Cf. SAINT THOMAS AQUINAS, "Peccator inveterascit, recedens a novitate Christi", *In Psalmos Davidis Lectura:* 6, 5.

105. *De Beatitudinibus,* Oratio VII: *PG* 44, 1280.

106. Cf. JOHN PAUL II, Encyclical Letter *Veritatis Splendor* (6 August 1993), 116: *AAS* 85 (1993), 1224.

107. Cf. JOHN PAUL II, Encyclical Letter *Centesimus Annus* (1 May 1991), 37: *AAS* 83 (1991), 840.

108. Cf. Message for Christmas 1967: *AAS* 60 (1968), 40.

109. PSEUDO-DIONYSIUS THE AREOPAGITE, *On the Divine Names,* 6, 1-3: *PG* 3, 856-857.

110. PAUL VI, *Pensiero alla Morte,* Istituto Paolo VI, Brescia 1988, 24.

111. JOHN PAUL II, Homily for the Beatification of Isidore Bakanja, Elisabetta Canori Mora and Gianna Beretta Molla (24 April 1994): *L'Osservatore Romano,* 25-26 April 1994, 5.

112. *Ibid.*

113. *In Matthaeum,* Hom. L, 3: *PG* 58, 508.

114. *Catechism of the Catholic Church,* No. 2372.

115. JOHN PAUL II, Address to the Fourth General Conference of Latin American Bishops in Santo Domingo (12 October 1992), No. 15: *AAS* 85 (1993), 819.

116. Cf. Decree on Ecumenism *Unitatis Redintegratio,* 12; Pastoral Constitution on the Church in the Modern World *Gaudium et Spes,* 90.

117. JOHN PAUL II, Post-Synodal Apostolic Exhortation *Familiaris Consortio* (22 November 1981), 17: *AAS* 74 (1982), 100.

118. Cf. SECOND VATICAN ECUMENICAL COUNCIL, Pastoral Constitution on the Church in the Modern World *Gaudium et Spes,* 50.

119. JOHN PAUL II, Encyclical Letter *Centesimus Annus* (1 May 1991), 39: *AAS* 83 (1991), 842.

120. JOHN PAUL II, Address to Participants in the Seventh Symposium of European Bishops, on the

theme of "Contemporary Attitudes towards Life and Death: a Challenge for Evangelization" (17 October 1989), No. 5: *Insegnamenti* XII, 2 (1989), 945. Children are presented in the Biblical tradition precisely as God's gift (cf. *Ps* 127:3) and as a sign of his blessing on those who walk in his ways (cf. *Ps* 128:3-4).

121. JOHN PAUL II, Encyclical Letter *Sollicitudo Rei Socialis* (30 December 1987), 38: *AAS* 80 (1988), 565-566.

122. JOHN PAUL II, Post-Synodal Apostolic Exhortation *Familiaris Consortio* (22 November 1981), 86: *AAS* 74 (1982), 188.

123. PAUL VI, Apostolic Exhortation *Evangelii Nuntiandi* (8 December 1975), 18: *AAS* 68 (1976), 17.

124. Cf. *ibid.*, 20: *loc. cit.*, 18.

125. Cf. SECOND VATICAN ECUMENICAL COUNCIL, Pastoral Constitution on the Church in the Modern World *Gaudium et Spes*, 24.

126. Cf. JOHN PAUL II, Encyclical Letter *Centesimus Annus* (1 May 1991), 17: *AAS* 83 (1991), 814; Encyclical Letter *Veritatis Splendor* (6 August 1993), 95-101: *AAS* 85 (1993), 1208-1213.

127. JOHN PAUL II, Encyclical Letter *Centesimus Annus* (1 May 1991), 24: *AAS* 83 (1991), 822.

128. JOHN PAUL II, Post-Synodal Apostolic Exhortation *Familiaris Consortio* (22 November 1981), 37: *AAS* 74 (1982), 128.

129. Letter establishing the World Day of the Sick (13 May 1992), No. 2: *Insegnamenti* XV, 1 (1992), 1410.

130. Cf. SECOND VATICAN ECUMENICAL COUNCIL, Pastoral Constitution on the Church in the Modern World *Gaudium et Spes*, 35; PAUL VI, Encyclical

Letter *Populorum Progressio* (26 March 1967), 15: *AAS* 59 (1967), 265.

131. Cf. JOHN PAUL II, Letter to Families *Gratissimam sane* (2 February 1994), 13: *AAS* 86 (1994), 892.

132. JOHN PAUL II, Motu Proprio *Vitae Mysterium* (11 February 1994), 4: *AAS* 86 (1994), 386-387.

133. *Closing Messages of the Council* (8 December 1965): *To Women.*

134. JOHN PAUL II, Apostolic Letter *Mulieris Dignitatem* (15 August 1988), 18: *AAS* 80 (1988), 1696.

135. Cf. JOHN PAUL II, Letter to Families *Gratissimam sane* (2 February 1994), 5: *AAS* 86 (1994), 872.

136. JOHN PAUL II, Address to Participants in the Study Conference on "The Right to Life in Europe" (18 December 1987): *Insegnamenti* X, 3 (1987), 1446.

137. *Message for the 1977 World Day of Peace: AAS* 68 (1976), 711-712.

138. BLESSED GUERRIC OF IGNY, *In Assumptione B. Mariae,* Sermo I, 2: *PL* 185, 188.

139. SECOND VATICAN ECUMENICAL COUNCIL, Dogmatic Constitution on the Church *Lumen Gentium,* 5.

140. Pastoral Constitution on the Church in the Modern World *Gaudium et Spes,* 22.

141. *Roman Missal,* Sequence for Easter Sunday.

142. SECOND VATICAN ECUMENICAL COUNCIL, Dogmatic Constitution on the Church *Lumen Gentium,* 68.

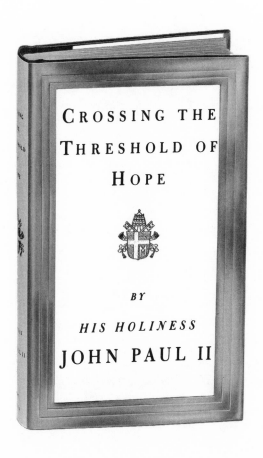

CROSSING THE
THRESHOLD OF
HOPE

BY

HIS HOLINESS

JOHN PAUL II

0-679-44084-4
$22.00 (Can: $30.00)

Available at your local bookstore
or wherever large print books are sold.
To receive a complete listing of large print titles
or to order directly, call
1-800-733-3000, or write to
Order Entry Department, Random House, Inc.
400 Hahn Road, Westminster, MD 21157

LM